Teaching Foreign Languages

An Historical Sketch

Renzo Titone

Georgetown University School of Languages and Linguistics

Teaching Foreign Languages

An Historical Sketch

Renzo Titone

Georgetown University Press, Washington, D.C. 20007

ACKNOWLEDGEMENTS

For all the friendly encouragement, the enlightening suggestions, and the editorial assistance granted me furing the final phase of this work I wish to thank Richard J. O'Brien, Neil J. Twombly, David R. Woods, and my students at the School of Languages and Linguistics, Georgetown University, Washington, D. C., for their stimulating interest in the topics developed in the following pages.

Renzo Titone, Director
Italian Center for Applied Linguistics
Rome, Italy

CONTENTS

INTRODUCTION   1

1   FOREIGN LANGUAGE TEACHING IN ANCIENT TIMES   4

The Sumerians   5
The Egyptians   6
The Romans   6

2   LANGUAGE TEACHING FROM THE RENAISSANCE TO 1800   8

Teaching in a practical way   8
Roger Ascham   10
William Bath   11
Wolfgang Ratke   11
Michel de Montaigne   12
Jan Amos Komensky   13
John Locke   15
César Dumarsais   16
Pierre Chompré   17
Ignatius Weitenauer   17
Johann Bernard Basedow   18
Claude-François Lysarde de Radonvilliers   19
P. J. F. Luneau de Boisgermain   20
James Hamilton   21
Joseph Jacotot   21

3   THE NINETEENTH CENTURY   26

Johann Heinrich Seidenstücker and Karl Plötz   27
Johann Franz Ahn and H. S. Ollendorf   28
Henry Wadsworth Longfellow   29
George Ticknor   30
Practical pioneers   31
Gottlieb Heness and L. Sauveur   31
Claude Marcel   32
François Gouin   33
Wilhelm Viëtor   37
Walter Ripman   38

4   HENRY SWEET   41

Sweet's life and orientation   41
General principles   43

Special principles   45
Evaluation of Sweet's contribution   48

5 OTTO JESPERSEN   50

General methodological orientation   51
Special principles   52
Evaluation of Jespersen's contribution   54

6 HAROLD E. PALMER   57

General methodological orientation   60
General principles   64
Special principles   68
Evaluation of Palmer's contribution   70

7 FOREIGN LANGUAGE TEACHING BEFORE WORLD WAR II   75

Report of the Committee of Twelve   75
François Closset and Adolf Bohlen   78
General Language and the Cleveland Plan   80
The Modern Foreign Language Study   82

8 FOREIGN LANGUAGE TEACHING TODAY   86

The United States   87
Great Britain   89
France   91
Germany   93
Canada   95
Italy   96
Spain   96
Holland   96
Philippine Islands   96
Classification of methods   97
    (1) The formal approach   97
    (2) The functional approach   99
        (a) The direct methods   100
        (b) The intensive method   106
        (c) The audiovisual method   107
        (d) The linguistic (-anthropological) method   108
        (e) The audio-lingual (aural-oral) method   109
    (3) The integrated approach   109
Conclusion   111

INTRODUCTION

The purpose of this historical summary is to help those interested in applied linguistics[1] to understand the various theoretical
and practical claims of contemporary language teaching methods
by critically reviewing past and present opinions and experiences
in this field. The general contents of this survey can be outlined
as follows:

(1) Ancient positions up to the sixteenth century: language
teaching from the origins of Western Civilization (Sumerians,
Egyptians, Greeks, and Romans) to the Renaissance in Western
Europe.

(2) Revival in modern European education from the sixteenth-
century scholar R. Ascham to the origins of the Direct Method
movement at the end of the nineteenth century.

(3) Contemporary trends: (a) Reactions against the grammar-
translation method, (b) Functional methods, and (c) Scientifically
integrated methods.

The following presentation of the developments in the field of
applied linguistics is based on an 'historical-comparative approach'. This approach is characterized mainly by the systematic comparison of facts and ideas in the two dimensions of time
and space. The thoughts of different times and places will be
examined in order to reach a critical understanding of the present
situation in the methodology of foreign language teaching.

The historical-comparative approach is significant in three
ways.

(1) History teaches us an important fact. Through a careful
consideration of the history of methodology we have come to
realize that the so-called 'traditional method' in language teaching is neither traditional nor classical but very recent. It dates

from a deviation in teaching method that came about at, or shortly before, the beginning of the nineteenth century. This deviation can most probably be explained by the inevitable lack of linguistic and psychological knowledge on the part of the language teachers in those days; and the traditional inertia or routine-addiction of the school practitioners, who did not care for change or improvement of their teaching habits.

(2) History gives us a perspective. A comparative view of parallel or past experiences can illustrate present trends in teaching. By comparing the new with the old, we better perceive the distinctive traits of today's language teaching methodology, which seems to be characterized by a new and more scientific orientation.

(3) History offers us a criterion. The historically-informed language teacher can adopt a more critical attitude vis-à-vis modern problems and solutions. He will have greater resourcefulness in finding and trying out solutions; he will not fall into naive repetition of out-moded procedures and unsuccessful attempts.

In order to grasp the significance of the historical approach fully, one must not think of the teacher as a mere handworker applying handed-down procedures mechanically, but rather as a skillful designer of the teaching process. The teacher should in fact follow certain steps in planning for better teaching. The following is a tentative enumeration:

(1) Understand the problem.
(2) Formulate pertinent hypotheses.
(3) Select one suitable hypothesis.
(4) Test the hypothesis.
(5) Apply it as a tentative solution.
(6) Re-test the solution and evaluate results on a larger scale.
(7) Improve the solution.

A genuine 'theory' can only be constructed after having reached the seventh step. What must be stressed here is that throughout these steps historical knowledge is a valuable guiding light, because the investigator must be guided and prompted by his store of previous experiences especially in formulating and selecting hypotheses.

Unfortunately, no complete monograph on the history of language teaching methods is yet available. The following is a list of publications containing at least one chapter on the subject: Closset (1953, chapter 1), Cochran (1958, part II), Kahl (1962),

Libbish (1964), Mallinson (1957, chapter 1), Newmark (1948), Titone (1965, chapter 6).

NOTE

[1] The author, throughout this work, understands by 'applied linguistics' not only the application of linguistic principles to language teaching, but an integrated methodology of language teaching based on such scientific disciplines as linguistics, anthropology, psychology, and scientific experimentation.

1

FOREIGN LANGUAGE TEACHING IN ANCIENT TIMES

The problem of finding and establishing a method of teaching foreign languages is relatively recent. It was not until the division of Europe at the end of the medieval era that certain vernaculars matured into national languages. Latin had been the lingua franca for some centuries throughout Europe. National fragmentation created linguistic boundaries that could only be surmounted by learning the newly-established tongues. Having to teach such languages posed a new problem, and this gave rise to an intellectual attitude that may be called 'method-consciousness'.

The necessity to communicate with foreign peoples, although never as critically and widely felt as today, is as old as the human race, or at least the tower of Babel! Military officials, diplomats, merchants of the past had to meet foreign populations and to exchange communications of various kinds.

How were foreign languages learned? Certainly not by theoretical study. Even though we may be surprised to find as perfect a grammar as the one compiled by the Indian Pāṇini (fourth century B.C.), we should note that such a grammar was obviously not meant to be a textbook for foreign students but was only a description of the native language for those more cultivated persons who wanted a deeper understanding of their own language.[1] Languages were learned through living contact with the peoples speaking them in their own environment. The process was, therefore, fairly similar to the one followed in learning the mother tongue.

It is interesting to recall how languages were taught by very ancient peoples like the Sumerians, the Egyptians, and the Romans.

The Sumerians

Fragmentary documents illustrating the way languages were taught in the remotest periods of human civilization can be found among the Sumerians. They were a clever and practical-minded people who preceded the Semites in governing the land first known as Sumer and later as Babylon. The civilization that they created between the fifth and the second millenium B.C. was probably the first great civilization on earth. Their ideas and literary works permeated the thought and the writings of all the peoples of Western Asia and to some extent also those of the Aegean world.

According to S. N. Kramer (1956, 1963), it would seem that since 3000 B.C. some scribes were devoted to school-teaching and learning. In 1902-03 a considerable number of school textbooks dating as far back as c. 2500 B.C. were unearthed in the old city of Shuruppak, the birthplace of the Sumerian 'Noah'. To a later period belong hundreds of clay tablets covered with all kinds of 'homework' laboriously done by young pupils. From these and other fragments left by the Sumerian teachers we can reconstruct a fairly complete picture of the Sumerian school, its trends, goals, students, teachers, curriculum, and teaching methods.

What goals were pursued in Sumerian education? The first aim was to teach prospective scribes how to make use of the cuneiform characters. Emphasis was placed on linguistic classification. Groups of interconnected words and phrases were memorized and then copied out by the students to the point of complete and satisfactory overlearning. In the Sumerian tablets we find that the study of grammar holds a distinctive place. Many tablets carry long lists of compound nouns and verbal forms which betray a surprisingly well developed analysis of grammar. But a more important fact is the development in second language teaching after the country of Sumer was conquered by the Akkadian Semites during the last quarter of the third millenium B.C. The Sumerian teachers had to teach their own language to their new lords, and they compiled the oldest known 'dictionaries'. The new conquerors adopted Sumeric writing, and guarded the literary inheritance of the Sumerians by continuing to study and imitate these works long after Sumeric was no longer spoken. Such intense study necessitated dictionaries, in which Sumerian words and expressions would appear in Akkadian translation. While grammatical classifications were used by the Sumerians in perfecting their knowledge of their own tongue, the Akkadians made use of bilingual dictionaries to learn Sumerian.

The Egyptians

Like the Akkadians, the Egyptians needed to know the languages of their conquered subjects. According to H. Brunner (1957, p. 98) 'that the Egyptians mastered foreign languages, at least during the empire of the 18th-20th Dynasties, cannot be doubted', as is clearly seen in the multilingual tablets contained in the Hamarna Archives.[2] The innumerable quotations of foreign words and phrases in the letters of the scribes during this period prove beyond doubt that they were familiar with the tongues of other countries. However, it is not known how foreign languages were studied. Brunner thinks, with good reason, that the young Egyptian bureaucrats used to be sent for their practical training to those countries where they were expected to work later on and became acquainted with foreign mores and languages. Hence it is probable that the bilingual tablets were of greater use to foreigners than to the Egyptians themselves.

The Romans

It should not sound astonishing when historians point out that a kind of 'direct method' was already used by the Romans to teach Greek to their children.[3] The education of the young Roman was bilingual from infancy. In his earlier years the child was entrusted to a Greek nurse or slave; when he reached school age, he would begin learning the three R's in the two languages at the same time; later on he would follow the parallel courses of the Greek grammaticós and of the Latin ludi magister, and then those given by the Greek rhetor and by the Latin orator. It was for this type of curriculum that the Roman teachers at the beginning of the third century A.D. worked out those curious bilingual manuals that were later called Hermeneumata Pseudodositheana. These manuals are comparable to our modern conversation handbooks and they appear in at least six different editions. They begin with a Greek-Latin vocabulary, first in alphabetical order, then semantically classified into capitula (chapters): there one finds names of gods and goddesses, of vegetables, fish, birds, and the like. There follows a series of very simple texts of a narrative or conversational character. Here is an example taken from a series of stories relating to the Emperor Hadrian:[4]

Petente quodam ut militaret,	Aitoûntos tínos hina strateuêsai,
Adrianus dixit:	Hadríanos eîpen·
'Ubi vis militare? ... '	'Pòs thelís strateúesthai; ... '

One also finds there some of Aesop's fables, an elementary handbook of mythology (the Genealogia by Iginius), a summary history
of the War of Troy and, more interestingly, a manual of daily
conversation, quotidiana conversatio (homilia kathemerinê), consisting of easy dialogues of a pleasant nature. The following[5] is
an example.

The paterfamilias moves toward his friend and says,
'Good morning, Caius', and he embraces him.
The latter returns the greeting and says,
'Nice to meet you. Would you like to come along?'
'Where?'
'To see our friend Lucius. We are going to pay him a visit. '
'What's the matter with him?'
'He's sick. '
'Since when?'
'Since a few days ago. '
'Where does he live?'
'Not very far from here. If you like we can go there. '
It was a quite practical way of teaching and, at the same time,
as can be seen from the above quotation, also a systematic
method which would tend to fix certain grammatical structures
in the learner's mind.

NOTES

[1] Pāṇini's grammar (entitled Astādhyāyī and consisting of
3,996 rules or aphorisms) is a true "science of words' (sab-
danusasana), that analyzes, describes, and classifies the elements and functions of the word. Cf. Boethlingk (1887) and
Renou (1948).
[2] Obviously the Egyptians could not trust foreign interpreters
alone. Cf. Hermann, Alfred (1956).
[3] We know that the Greeks, on the contrary, were not inclined
to study the languages of the so-called 'barbarians' (barbaros) so
that, even in later times, in Hellenistic education, 'fremde
Sprachen ... fehlten völlig'. Nilsson (1955:11).
[4] Corpus Glossariorum Latinorum III, 31, 24 ff.
[5] Ibid. 647, 4; 649, 6. Author's translation.

2

LANGUAGE TEACHING FROM THE RENAISSANCE TO 1800

One may immediately ask why nothing is said of the Middle Ages: was not foreign language teaching in medieval times a problem? The answer is as immediate as the query: in those days the international language of communication and culture throughout Europe was Latin, and this was part and parcel of the common curriculum from the elementary grades to the university. The medieval educated man was bilingual. Latin was taught intensively like the mother tongue, at least up until the Renaissance period. Latin was still a living language, and it was taught in a living way, first orally and then through reading and composition. When the preoccupation with teaching modern languages made itself felt in the Renaissance, modern languages were taught in a direct, intensive manner. But in later centuries when Latin, as a dead tongue, was confined to grammars and dictionaries, modern languages were also treated in a bloodless fashion.

Teaching in a practical way

The practical way languages were taught from the sixteenth century on is worth considering. In those days, learning a foreign language, usually French, was considered an important part of a nobleman's education. Toward the end of the following century this practice was also introduced into the upper middle class, and English was added to French. The aim of language study was essentially practical: to acquire the ability to get along in the ordinary circumstances of daily life. No reference, therefore, was made either to literature or to grammar. Nor was grammar conceived as a means of mental training. The only

norm was the immediate utility that mastery of a foreign language could bring into social intercourse, business relations, or
foreign travels (cf. Lehmann 1904: 8 f and 12 f).

As a consequence, the method of learning was essentially practical and did not undergo any change for a few centuries. As living languages, foreign languages were to be absorbed in a living
way, through direct contact with foreign people (head stewards,
servants, nurses), in hotels and during travels. This would ensure the young man a direct knowledge also of the people and
customs of the foreign country. Obviously, such an acquaintance
with all aspects of a foreign culture would also mold the understanding and attitudes of the young learner, thus contributing to
the enrichment of his personality (cf. Bohl 1928: 524).

The teachers as a rule were native speakers of the language.
The interaction between teacher and pupil would take the form of
a true-to-life situation in which communicative behavior would
be conditioned by an over-all foreign pattern. The teaching
method would consist primarily in conversation practice following more or less the following stages: (a) first the teacher would
talk and the pupil would listen attentively; (b) then, the pupil
would receive brief explanations about what had been said: often
enough these brief explanations would be presented mimically or
in the foreign language itself; (c) finally, the pupil was expected
to imitate what he had heard from the instructor, even though the
meaning of it was not entirely clear. The instructor's primary
emphasis was laid on oral work; repeated imitation and occasional
reading would ensure the pupil a sufficiently firm grasp of the
sound chains of the foreign speech.[1] The pupil was expected to
make every effort to speak without worrying too much about his
mistakes which would be corrected by his tutor. Grammatical
forms would thus be assimilated through practice.[2] When shy-
ness prevented a pupil from imitating by ear, he would be forced
to memorize certain reading texts taken from several existing
conversation handbooks dealing with daily situations.[3]

Inevitably such teaching procedures entailed certain defects.
First, the strict memory approach confined the student to ready-
made expressions without enabling him to master the language
freely. Second, the language spoken by the native instructors
was not always a standard form. Third, the vocabulary store
was generally rather limited in quality and extent. Recognizing
such limitations, some teachers with a philological background
began to prepare suitable textbooks and readers.[4]

One noteworthy characteristic, however, was that both the instructors and the new textbooks made little or no use of the pupil's mother tongue. Perhaps the first time that any connection was made between the first and the second language was in an English-German grammar by H. Offelen (1687). The author explained English sounds by comparing them with similar German sounds and presented bilingual lists of words characterized by close formal similarity.[5]

It is clear that the practical method employed by these native instructors was very much like the later so-called 'direct method'. These conditions lasted until new developments in the theoretical approach came about at the beginning of the nineteenth century.

Together with the current practices illustrated above, the historian can notice a certain trend in educational thought that favored the use of direct procedures. A number of educators from the sixteenth to the eighteenth century held opinions about the methods of language teaching that appear strikingly modern.

The way the Latin language was still taught in the best schools of this period became the model of foreign language instruction. The trend was to teach elementary Latin first by means of intensive oral practice on the basis of conversation handbooks like the famous Dialogi or Colloquia compiled by such authorities as Heyden, Cordier, Fr. Van Torre, S.J. These had bilingual texts made up of familiar expressions and used vernacular translation in interlinear or parallel fashion.[6] Only later were the pupils introduced to grammar.

Roger Ascham

Roger Ascham (1515-68) outlined his method of teaching Latin in his guide, The Scholemaster (posthumous, 1570). He took as a basic textbook a selection of Cicero's Epistolae. The teacher began by translating the first letter and repeated his translation until the pupil had grasped the meaning of each word. Then the pupil tried the same translation in writing. After this the same pupil re-translated the text back into Latin without referring to the original and then compared his translation with the original Latin and corrected his mistakes. Grammar also was to be taught on the basis of the texts. A French historian, Compayré, comments on Ascham's method as follows: 'La comparaison des thèmes de l'élève avec un texte latin original est un des traits essentiels du système d'Ascham. La traduction est l'exercise

le plus utile, mais surtout la double traduction, celle que Pline
le Jeune recommandait deja: "Ex Graeco in Latinum, vel ex
Latino in Graecum" (Ep. VII, 9)' (Compayré, 1880: 119).

William Bath

Suggestive of a broader comparative approach is the work of
the Irish Jesuit, William Bath (1564-1614), more commonly known
under the Latinized form of his name, Bateus.[7] At the Irish College in Salamanca he started the composition of his Latin-Spanish
Janua linguarum (Gate to languages) that was completed later with
the aid of his confreres. The book was first published in
Salamanca in 1611. It contains 1200 proverbial sentences embodying the most frequently used Latin words. The Latin text is faced
by the Spanish translation. An appendix follows these sentences,
entitled De ambiguis, which presents sentences composed with
Latin homonyms, e.g. Dum malum comedis juxta malum navis,
de malo commisso sub malo vetita meditare 'While you eat an
apple by the ship mast, think over the evil committed under the
forbidden apple tree'. The book closes with an alphabetical index
of all the Latin words used throughout the texts. Each word is
numbered to refer to the sentence in which that word appeared.
In 1615 an English translation of the Janua was issued. Success
spread. In 1617, the Janua was published in a quadrilingual edition, Janua Linguarum quadrilinguis (Latin, English, French,
and Spanish). Finally, in 1630, a six-language edition appeared
in Strasbourg, Janua Linguarum silinguis. We can conclude,
therefore, that Bath's conception of language learning was essentially vocabulary learning, but the vocabulary items were always
learned and memorized in context.

Wolfgang Ratke

Ascham's emphasis on translation as a teaching procedure was
shared to some extent at least as a methodological starting point,
by the German educator, Wolfgang Ratke or Ratichius (1571-1635).
Ratke taught Latin by using Terence's plays as texts. Before beginning to teach grammar, he would always give a good translation of each text. His chief didactic principles can be found in
his book, Memorial (1612):
(1) Teach each point in an orderly manner and following the
natural course of things.

(2) Do not teach everything at the same time, but each thing at the right time.

(3) Repeat the points you have taught regularly.

(4) Do not learn by heart.

(5) Make things uniform: for example, unify the grammar of different languages on one same plan or pattern.

(6) First the thing in itself should be known, then—and only then—according to its modalities (ne modus rei ante rem).

(7) Everything should be learned through experience and induction.

Ratke and Ascham have several methodological views in common: the initial presentation of a basic text and the derivation of grammar rules from the texts. As Quick rightly observed: 'When we compare Ratke's method with Ascham's, we find several points of agreement. Ratke would begin the study of a language by taking a model book, and working through it with the pupil a great many times. Ascham did the same. Each lecture according to his plan would be gone over "a dozen times at the least". Both construed to the pupil instead of requiring him to make out the sense for himself. Both Ratke and Ascham taught grammar not by itself, but in connection with the model book' (Quick 1907: 117). The appeal made to experience and induction is strikingly modern, but more will be said about it by other outstanding educationists like Comenius.

Michel de Montaigne

The French essayist Michel de Montaigne (1533-92) occupies a place apart. He experienced personally the practical language instruction given in those days; but at the same time he entertained a philosophy of language teaching which was consistent with the practice of his day. It is also enlightening for the modern methodologist. We read in one of Montaigne's essays: 'En nourrice et avant le premier dénouement de la langue, mon père me donna en charge à un Allemand ... du tout ignorant de notre langue, et très bien versé en la Latine. Celui-ci ... m'avait continuellement entre les bras. Il y en eut aussi avec lui deux autres moindres en savoir pour me suivre, et soulager le premier. Ceux-ci ne m'entretenaient d'autre langue que la Latine. Quant au reste de sa maison, c'était une règle inviolable que ni lui-même, ni ma mère, ni valet, ni chambrière, ne parlaient en ma compagnie qu'autant de mots de Latin que chacun avait appris pour jargonner avec moi ... Et sans art, sans livre, sans

grammaire ou précepte, sans fouet et sans larmes, j'avais appris
du Latin, tout aussi pur que mon maître d'école le savait' (Villey
1922: 223).

This training in Latin was less intensive in the Collège de
Guyenne, where Montaigne was sent at the age of six. There,
Latin was no longer spoken as a living tongue, and he soon lost
his ability to converse in it. The essay, from which we have
taken the above quotation, is all the more significant, given the
time of its first publication (1580), because of Montaigne's insistence on the necessity of learning the language through direct
contact with its native speakers, and getting acquainted with the
mind, customs, and culture of the foreign people. He says that
by far the best way to educate a young noble is to cause him to
seek 'le commerce des hommes' by visiting foreign countries,
'non pour en rapporter seulement ... combien le visage de Néron,
de quelque vieille reine de là, est plus long ou plus large que
celui de quelque pareille médaille, mais pour en rapporter principalement les humeurs de ces nations et leurs façons, et pour
frotter et limer notre cervelle contre celle d'autrui' (Villey 1922:
196). Montaigne's idea represents the embryonic concept of the
modern so-called 'area studies' that are supposed to integrate
knowledge of the language with knowledge of the country.

Jan Amos Komensky

The greatest educationist of the seventeenth century was the
Czech, Jan Amos Komensky, or Comenius (1592-1670). His name
is linked forever with his greatest work, the Didactica Magna
(1568), a treatise on the universal way of successful teaching.
He was not, however, only interested in the general philosophy
of the teaching process, but also showed a keen interest in the
problems of language teaching. In fact, he may be considered a
pioneer of the 'direct method', inasmuch as he succeeded in
formulating clearly certain principles of language teaching which
he recognized as fundamental and applied extensively, and which
are among the bases of even today's methodology. Most of these
principles are summed up in Comenius' greatest work, Didactica
Magna, but they were first put forth and amply illustrated in
three other didactical works.

Comenius was inspired by Bath's Janua linguarum to compose
his own Janua linguarum reserata aurea 'The golden gate to languages unlocked' (1631). The main object of this book is to teach
Latin. It contains about eight thousand words in common usage,

grouped into different classifications. These words were eventually used in a series of sentences, at first quite easy but gradually increasing in complexity. It was the first kind of basic dictionary. But the words were not isolated. Each Latin sentence was accompanied by its vernacular translation in a facing column. He soon realized, however, that this manual was rather difficult for the ordinary pupil, and he tried new and more practical methods.

Called to Sweden in 1642 to help with school reform there, Comenius further perfected his method. Language learning was to be made easier and more effective by insisting more systematically upon the principal of intuition, nihil est in intellectu quin prius fuerit in sensu 'nothing can become a concept of the intellect unless it has been first a sensory percept'. He developed this thesis in a treatise published in 1648, Methodus linguarum novissima (A new method of studying languages) which heralded a series of textbooks designed to facilitate the teaching of Latin and to adapt the materials of the Janua linguarum. In these class manuals the principle of 'think, speak, act' is clearly enunciated and applied. The leading principle of the so-called 'intuitive method' is condensed in this statement to be found in his Methodus linguarum novissima: 'Pictures are what most easily impress themselves in a child's mind, to remain lasting and real. Children need to be given many examples, and things they can see, and not abstract rules of grammar'.

The use of sensory experience as an intuitive starting point for teaching was still more definitely and practically developed in a third work by Comenius. It was during a stay in Hungary (1650-54), where he had been called by Prince Rakoczy to found a model school, that he wrote the Orbis sensualium pictus (The world in pictures), published in 1658. In his preface to this book, Comenius maintained that the constant concern must be that the child should see nothing that he could not put a name to, and that he should name nothing without being able to point to it. With this manual Comenius introduced illustrations into school textbooks —not primarily for adornment but to fulfil a definite purpose, and became the first to maintain the pedagogical principle that in all language teaching the first appeal must be to sense perception.

The great synthesizing precept that remains as Comenius' most characteristic guiding principle is the emphasis on practice in language learning: Omnis lingua usu potius discatur quam praeceptis 'Every language must be learned by practice rather than by rules, especially by reading, repeating, copying, and by written and oral attempts at imitation'.[8]

John Locke

The English philosopher John Locke (1632-1704) seems to carry on the tradition of Ascham on the one hand and of Montaigne and Comenius on the other. As far as the written language is concerned, he follows Ascham's method, but he adds something new—interlinear translation. Latin and English lines run one on top of the other. Lateral arrangement, as used by Bath and Comenius, is replaced by interlinear arrangement. Locke took as a basic text Aesop's fables, deriving from it all the rules of grammar.[9]

But a more practical slant is to be found in the work published by Locke toward the end of his life, Some Thoughts Concerning Education (1693), where he betrayed the influence of both Montaigne and Comenius, condemning the grammatical method of teaching Latin and the foolishness and pedantry of schoolmasters in general. Like Montaigne he is all for the 'natural' method of learning a foreign tongue, and he recommends French as a second language, to be 'talked into' the child.

When he can speak and read French well, which in this Method is usually in a Year or two, he should proceed to Latin, which 'tis a wonder Parents, when they have had the experiment in French, should not think ought to be learned in the same way, by talking and reading ... If therefore a Man could be got, who himself speaking good Latin, would always be about your Son, talk constantly to him, and suffer him to speak or read nothing else, this would be the true and genuine way ... If such a Man cannot be got, who speaks good Latin ... the next best thing is to have him taught as near this way as may be, which is by taking some easy and pleasant Book, such as Aesop's Fables, and writing the English Translation (made as literal as it can be) in one Line, and the Latin words which answer each of them, just over it in another ... This being a more imperfect Way than by talking Latin unto him; the Formation of the Verbs first, and afterwards the Declensions of the Nouns and Pronouns perfectly learned by Heart, may facilitate his Acquaintance with the Genius and Manner of the Latin Tongue ... More than this

of Grammar, I think he need not have ... For Languages
are only to be learned by rote; and a Man who does not
speak English or Latin perfectly by rote, so that having
thought of the thing he would speak of, his Tongue of
Course, without Thought of Rule or Grammar, falls into
the proper Expression and Idiom of that Language, does
not speak it well, nor is Master of it. And I would fain
have any one name to me that Tongue, that any one can
learn, or speak as he should do, by the Rules of Grammar. Languages were not made by Rules or Art, but by
Accident, and the common Use of the People. And he that
will speak them well, has no other Rule but that; nor any
thing to trust to, but his Memory, and the Habit of speaking after the Fashion learned from those, that are allowed
to speak properly, which in other Words is only to speak
by rote ... If Grammar ought to be taught at any time, it
must be to one that can speak the Language already; how
else can he be taught the Grammar of it? (Quick 1880:
134-48).

Locke's words might have been written over one century later.

César Dumarsais

In France, since the beginning of the eighteenth century, we
notice a growing tendency to revise educational methods. In
other countries, like Germany and England, attempts at reform
had started earlier. But the French reform was mainly the work
of humble educators whose names are scarcely mentioned in the
treatises on the history of education. One of these was César
Dumarsais (1676-1756) who was perhaps the first to think out
more efficient ways of teaching. He was ranked by Voltaire
among those 'sages obscurs, qui jugent sainement de tout, qui
vivent entre eux dans la paix et la communication de la raison,
ignorés des grands et redoutés de ces charlatans en tous génies
qui veulent dominer sur tous les exprits' (Michaud 1885: 504).
In the biographical encyclopedia, Biographie universelle, compiled by Michaud, we read with reference to Dumarsais the following statement: 'Ses contemporains le méconnurent, son plus
bel ouvrage resta trente ans dans les magasins du libraire, et ce
ne fut qu'un demi-siècle après sa mort qu'une compagnie savante
daigna jeter quelques fleurs sur sa tombe' (Michaud 1885: 505).

Dumarsais expounds his method and ideas in his book, Exposition d'une méthode raisonnée pour apprendre la langue latine (1722). His method is easy and natural. Languages are learned by use. Those who want to learn a language must first of all use their memory; they will have to learn first the most commonly used words. If they want to learn Latin, they must have a text where the Latin translation is on the line running over the vernacular text. Comparison between the Latin and the vernacular texts is the main feature of this type of study. By proceeding from interlinear translation toward a good translation, and from this back to the original text, the pupil will be able to understand 'le jeu des traductions et le génie de la langue'. Dumarsais took Horace's Carmen saeculare and Juvenal's Epitome de diis et de heroibus as basic textbooks for teaching Latin. The original text, the interlinear translation, and the acceptable version were printed in different types so as to impress their different roles on the pupil. [10] Latin was almost a dead language at that time, and yet some educators wanted to have it taught like any living tongue.

Pierre Chompré

Preoccupations similar to Dumarsais' were shared by another contemporary French educator, Pierre Chompré (1698-1760). Although his Dictionaire de la fable (1727) is better known, two other booklets have greater relevance for us, namely his Moyen d'apprendre les langues et principalement la latine (1757) and Essai de feuilles élémentaires pour apprendre le latin sans grammaire ni dictionnaire (1768, posthumous). These publications are important first because of the direct approach used in teaching Latin and other languages, and second because Chompré seems to have inspired a famous French scholar, Jacotot, of whom more later, [11] as well as other educators.

Ignatius Weitenauer

While the new educational trend was developing with Dumarsais in France, the Jesuit Ignatius Weitenauer (1705-83) was writing his book Hexaglotton (1762) in Germany. [12] His method went beyond the traditional teaching of Latin and extended to twelve languages. It used a comparative approach and interlinear translation. It was also supposed to be an intensive method, for, by following his study procedures, one could learn a foreign language in a few lessons: 'Nulla harum (linguarum) fuit in qua non intra alteram tertiamve horam, Deo dante, audientem eo perducerem, ut interpretari libros per se ipse, et ope lexici explicare debet (1762:5)'. His teaching method is expounded in his Hexaglotton, which comprises five brief sections for each language:

(1) A brief grammatical summary should first be memorized. Such a grammar is composed according to an identical pattern for each language.

(2) A brief basic vocabulary (spicilegium) containing the words used throughout the text.

(3) A list of particles, especially those used in compound verbs.

(4) A demonstration to show how, by making use of the preceding aids, one can translate and explain a text. (By means of figures placed on top of each word the author refers to the grammar, the vocabulary, and the particle list.)

(5) An appendix dealing with pronunciation. (It is interesting to find here a sample of interlinear phonetic transcription of the text used for the demonstration.)

Latin is still the basic language from which the paradigms of the others are derived. The text used for Latin is a modern narrative taken from Fenelon's Télémaque.

In Weitenauer's manual, the study of the written language was no longer the exclusive object of instruction, and concern for oral learning was becoming so prominent as to lead the author to care for accurate pronunciation. (Weitenauer's appendix on pronunciation is perhaps the first attempt at using phonetic transcription, although in an approximate manner and with reference to the Latin graphic system.) No less original is the contribution offered by Weitenauer's four preliminary sections to a more accurate study of the texts. We realize that with this author methodology is coming of age; procedures are being gradually refined and the means are better suited to the instructional objectives of language teaching.

Johann Bernard Basedow

During the same time, in Germany educational reform was having its heyday. More celebrated than Weitenauer for his wider educational enterprise, was a talented if erratic young German, Johann Bernard Basedow (1723-90). At the age of twenty-six he accepted the position of tutor to the children of a Holstein family, learned French by conversing with a French governess, and employed a similar technique, using Comenius' Orbis pictus as his textbook, to teach Latin to the son of the house. Several writings on his methods and ideas about teaching languages and natural science made him known, but his fame was due mainly to his founding of the Philanthropinum, a training college for teachers and a boarding school for children from six to eighteen years. In 1774 Prince Leopold of Dessau had called Basedow to his principality and had entrusted him with the task of reorganizing the school system. His experimental Philanthropinum could be compared to a modern 'experimental school' attached to a university school of education. The crowning glory of Basedow's institution came in 1776 when, before a vast audience drawn from all over Germany, he and his associates gave a demonstration examination of the children they had taught, to prove how efficient their methods were.[13] His aim was to form Europeans and world citizens and to prepare them for as happy and as useful an existence as possible. More realistic than the belated spokesmen of literary humanism he drew inspiration from Comenius and Rousseau's Emile, thus emphasizing the necessity of following nature. His practical sense also influenced his ideas concerning the teaching of languages. Languages were to be taught by speaking and then by reading, and grammar was not to be introduced until late in the course. While Latin was not to be neglected, more attention was to be paid to the mother tongue and to French. Facility in the language was to be acquired through conversation, games, pictures, drawing, acting plays, and reading on practical and interesting subjects.

In France, meanwhile, interest in effective teaching of Latin went hand in hand with concern for efficient ways of teaching the modern languages. France was producing other representatives of the 'new breed' in education. Though not widely known in the history of education, they deserve thoughtful consideration and recognition for their work. With these educators, the primary emphasis was still on direct understanding of the text (explication de texte) by means of interlinear translation, not grammar.

Claude-François Lysarde de Radonvilliers

Claude-François Lysarde de Radonvilliers (1709-89), an assistant tutor to the children of Louis XV, favored the traditional use of interlinear translation, but defined the aim of this procedure: 'La seule chose essentielle est de joindre toujours un mot connu au mot inconnu, afin qu'en lisant un livre, écrit dans une langue qu'on ne sait pas, on entende cependant les mots de la pensée de l'auteur' (1768:xi). Radonvilliers aimed at teaching several langauges. In fact, he gives an example in his book De la manière d'apprendre les langues which is quite comparable to Weitenauer's Hexaglotton. It deals with such languages as Greek, German, English, Spanish, and Italian. Radonvilliers' comparative approach does not favor a word-for-word translation and comparison of isolated elements in the native and foreign tongue, but wants each word taken in its proper context so that the author's thought might be understood.

P. J. F. Luneau de Boisgermain

Convinced of the truth of Radonvilliers' precepts, P. J. F. Luneau de Boisgermain (1732-1804) tried to put them to wider use. He published a series of textbooks for studying foreign languages: Cours de langue italienne (1783, 3 vols.), Cours de langue latine (1798, 5 vols.), and Cours de langue anglaise (1784-87, 2 vols.). In this latter course he applied the device of interlinear translation to Fenelon's Télémaque. Luneau de Boisgermain claims that by following his method a student would be able to learn a foreign language in a short time without the aid of a teacher. His ideas on the use of grammar are clearly negative, and he tends to emphasize direct practice. He states: 'J'ai dit qu'on apprend partout la langue que l'on parle sans secours de la grammaire, qui lui est propre. J'ai dit qu'on n'a pensé à faire des grammaires d'une langue que quand elle a été perfectionnée' (1783:x). The idea of the dominant role of practice is again emphasized by the author when he speaks of the role of the teacher in foreign language work. He says:

> Quant on veut étudier une langue, je pense qu'il faut se conduire comme on conduit un enfant auquel on veut apprendre à parler sa langue maternelle; et qu'il faut suivre dans cette nouvelle étude l'instinct seul des mères qui apprennent a parler à leurs enfants. Quand la nature a donné aux organes de l'enfant la facilité d'articuler les sons differents de la voix, une mère lui apprend les mots de sa langue, les uns après les autres. Elle les lui répète jusqu'à ce qu'il les ait retenus et qu'il en fasse usage. Les mères n'emploient pour cela ni maîtres ni

grammaires. Elles parlent à leurs enfants: elles leur
mettent des mots dans la mémoire. Je veux qu'on fasse
comme elles, quand on veut apprendre une langue étran-
gère ... Messieurs les maîtres de langues étrangères ne
voient dans l'étude des langues que la prononciation et la
grammaire. Ils sont intéressés à donner beaucoup
d'importance à ce travail (1783:xv).

Boisgermain was the first to define so concretely the idea of
the 'natural method'.

James Hamilton

The tendency to do away with grammar in language study is
common to all those in this period who maintain that languages
are best learned through some sort of 'natural' method, namely
by conversation or comparison between first and second language.
This same conviction can be found in an English spokesman of
the educational reform, James Hamilton (1769-1831). He was at
heart a very practical man and came to language teaching through
his own experience. Hamilton wanted to establish his business in
Hamburg, Germany, and accordingly he had to learn the German
language. He went to see an immigrant, a French general by the
name of D'Angeli, who was teaching without grammar by translating word for word the text of a little collection of German
anecdotes. After a dozen lessons, Hamilton claimed, he could
already understand an easy little book in German. This experience lies at the root of the 'Hamilton method'. Nothing is entirely new in this method. Hamilton teaches by making use of
interlinear translation. As a starting point he took St. John's
Gospel and began translating it in front of his pupils word by
word. His pupils were expected to repeat this exercise after him
and then they would translate the same text aloud or in writing
until their translation was perfect.
These simple procedures are presented by Hamilton in his
book, Essay on the Usual Mode of Teaching Language (New York,
1816). Some years later he published an account of his experiences in teaching languages with his method.[14]

Joseph Jacotot

The ideas and practices of the educators encountered so far
can be found synthesized in the work of Joseph Jacotot (1770-1840),

a French reformer who drew abundantly from them. Jacotot had an unusually rich teaching experience. A lawyer at the age of nineteen and then a <u>docteur ès lettres</u>, he was called to teach at the Collège des Godrans in Dijon in 1791. In 1794 he became assistant director of the École Polytechnique in Paris and a year later professor of logic and of the 'analysis of sensations and ideas' (psychology) at the École Centrale of Dijon. Teacher of classical languages in the same school, of mathematics at the Lycée of Dijon (1804), of Roman Law at the Faculté de Droit of Dijon (1806), professor of mathematics at the new Faculté des Sciences of Dijon and then associate member of the Académie des Sciences et des Belles-Lettres of his native town, he was, for his days, a sort of 'walking encyclopedia'. An exile in Belgium during the second restoration of the Bourbons, he settled in Brussels and later in Louvain. In 1818, he was named lecturer of French at the University of Louvain, where he thought out his famous method of 'universal teaching' (<u>méthode de l'enseignement universel</u>). His method was at first favorably and rather widely accepted, but then it became controversial. Followers and adversaries fought in long oral and written debates. Two parties came into existence: the 'jacotins' and the 'antijacotins'.

The most important of Jacotot's works are <u>Enseignement universel</u>, <u>Langue maternelle</u> (1823), <u>Enseignement universel, Langue étrangère</u> (1830), <u>Enseignement universel, Musique, Dessein et Peinture</u> (1824), <u>Enseignement universel, Mathématiques</u> (1841), <u>Enseignement universel, Droit et Philosophie panécastique</u>, and <u>Enseignement universel, Mélanges posthumes</u> (1841).

Jacotot's method, applicable to the teaching of all knowledge, can be summed up in one fundamental proposition: 'Il faut apprendre quelque chose et y rapporter tout le reste'.

The idea applied by Jacotot is a distinct echo of Comenius in his <u>Great Didactics</u>—to find the method that would enable any teacher to teach anything to any pupil. But, unlike Comenius, he would emphasize the organic character of knowledge whereby new notions could be deduced from previously acquired knowledge. The above proposition would then be made explicit through the following teaching stages:

(1) To learn something new means that:
    (a) one must first memorize a complex unit ('un tout') which will serve as a basis;
    (b) the memorized text will have to be repeated regularly;

(c) it should be further studied by reflection, analysis, and trying to 'squeeze out' the largest number of implicit notions;

(d) by means of questions and comparisons the learned material will be tested in order to ensure a deep assimilation of it.

(2) Whatever has been newly learned must always be linked with what was already known.

Jacotot's method has been called an 'analytic-synthetic method of concentration' (Geerts and Missinne 1964: 546), inasmuch as its essential procedures consist in grasping a whole (global approach), analyzing it or breaking it down into its components (analysis), and finally recomposing it into an organic synthesis. At the beginning, it was meant to be used for teaching reading and foreign languages, but it can easily be applied to teaching any subject—as Jacotot actually did. Hence, a 'method of universal teaching'.

Let us examine more carefully Jacotot's application of his method to the teaching of foreign languages. His usual starting point was a basic reader. For the study of Latin, it was the Epitome historiae sacrae, and for the other languages the text of Fenelon's Télémaque. Here the original text is faced by a literal translation. The pupil sets out to memorize a long passage and repeats it as often as needed. With the aid of the literal translation he comes to grasp the meaning of each word, while his analysis of the whole sentence enables him to deduce certain implicit grammar rules. Of course, this procedure demands a great number of oral and written exercises in which the pupil imitates, summarizes, and compares the texts. Everything that the pupil acquires in this fashion must be linked to his preceding notions by his comparing similarities and differences between the new and the old.

Jacotot's chief methodological principle can be translated into another more condensed proposition: 'Tout est dans tout'. Nothing is entirely new; everything pre-exists in certain basic nuclei of knowledge that need only be made explicit through induction and deduction. All notions making up a field of science can be deduced from a small core of knowledge, if it is submitted to minute analysis.

Jacotot's originality has been disputed, and there is sufficient proof that apart from certain new formulae and interesting practical applications, most of his teaching principles are actually the 'best' educational contributions made by most of the seventeenth- and eighteenth-century reformers.

But the good tradition established in these two centuries was soon to be spoiled as new 'deviating' trends showed up during the first half of the nineteenth century.

NOTES

[1] This procedure is shown by Laurent Chifflets in his Grammaire Françoise written entirely in French: this was widely used also in Germany during the second half of the seventeenth century.

[2] This appears from a conversation in the French grammar by Nathaniel Duezs, which first came out in French (1635), then in Latin (1647), and finally in German (1656). It was reprinted into the eighteenth century.

[3] The first of the kind is the one entitled Manière de langages which appeared in 1693 handwritten by Canon M. T. Coyfurelly of Orléans. Contents: chief conversation forms, letter models, love letters in poetry, etc. Lehmann (1904) presents a whole series of such manuals published later.

[4] These are mainly brief grammatical summaries, especially containing paradigms of declensions and conjugations, with appended dialogues, word derivations, topical classifications of nouns, etc.

[5] At the beginning of the nineteenth century, the first grammar books would become a mere transposition of the Latin grammatical patterns described by Donatus to the analysis of modern languages.

[6] Cf. Woodward (1924); Cubberly (1920) and (1948); Ganss (1956); all contain valuable information regarding the teaching of Latin in the sixteenth and seventeenth century schools in France and Germany.

[7] Concerning his life, cf. Aug. et Al. De Backer, et C. Sommervogel, 1890, column 1009. His method of teaching languages has been described by Quick (1907:160-63).

[8] Comenius' original contribution to the intuitive method is unanimously recognized. 'C'est vraiment Comenius qui, le premier, eut l'idée d'une pédagogie fondée sur l'intuition sensible. Il en a ouvert la féconde tradition dans les pays germaniques où jusqu'à ces derniers temps, elle a été dominante. Comenius continue Luther; c'est pour lui une façon d'adorer le Créateur que de saisir la création par les sens et par l'esprit. Mais il se

rattache aussi à la philosophie sensualiste et affirme à son tour que toute connaissance est d'abord sensible et que rien n'est dans l'esprit qui n'ait d'abord été dans les sens.' (Leif and Rustin 1953: 271-2). Leif and Rustin's statements are typical of a one-sided historical interpretation, where the fact (Comenius' originality) is easily recognized, but the origins of the fact are too facilely traced to certain biased sources. Comenius' realism stems not so much from Luther or from the sensualist philosophers as from his basic Christian recognition of the totality of the spiritual-material world and from the common trend of his times towards a more concrete concept of language (res et verba: words have meaning in so far as they retain their natural connection with reality).

[9] 'He advocated teaching foreign languages without grammar, and he published: Aesop's Fables in English and Latin, interlineary. For the benefit of those who not having a master, would learn either of these tongues.' (Quick 1907: 238). Cf. Leroy (1863:243).

[10] 'Dumarsais appartient à la catégorie des pédagogues plus ingénieux que profonds qui, respectant et conservant dans la vieille éducation les objets de l'enseignement, s'efforcent seulement d'en faciliter l'accès et d'en abréger la route.' (Compayré 1880: II, p. 138). Most of the teachers questioned by the Ministry of National Education in France in 1799 answered that 'ils employaient la méthode de Dumarsais pour l'enseignement des langues anciennes'. Archives nationales de France, F 17 1342.

[11] In the Public Library of Dijon, V. M. Geerts and L. Missinne found a manuscript which testifies that Jacotot knew well Chompré's and Dumarsais' publications. Cf. Geerts and Missinne (1964:553).

[12] The complete title was: Hexaglotton sive modus addiscendi intra brevissimum tempus linguas: gallicam, italicam, hispanicam, graecam, hebraicam, chaldaicam, anglicam, germanicam, belgicam, latinam, lusitaneam et syricam.

[13] Cf. Goethe's poem, 'Diner zu Koblenz im Sommer' (1774):
    'Zwischen Lavater und Basedow
    Sass ich bei Tisch ...
    Prophete rechts, Prophete links,
    Das Weltkind in der Mitten.'

[14] The title of his second book is: The History, Principles, Practice and Results of the Hamilton System for the Last 12 Years, Manchester, 1829.

3

THE NINETEENTH CENTURY

Two opposing currents may be seen in language learning between the Renaissance and 1800. The best educational practice
in these centuries was along the lines of common sense, not yet
infected by the virus of formal 'grammaticalism'; that is, it was
still common practice to teach languages by living contact with
them, whether in their oral or their written form. The second
trend in language teaching after the Renaissance had already begun to be formalized in a systematic teaching of grammar based
on paradigms, tables, declensions and conjugations. One can
easily agree with V. Mallinson about the cause of this deviation,
when he writes: 'When once the Latin tongue had ceased to be a
normal vehicle for communication, and was replaced as such by
the vernacular languages, then it most speedily became a "mental gymnastic", the supremely "dead" language, a disciplined
and systematic study of which was held to be indispensable as a
basis for all forms of higher education. Classical studies were
then intended and made to produce an excellent mental discipline,
a fortitude of spirit and a broad humane understanding of life.
They succeeded triumphantly for the times in their objective.
And when under the pressure of circumstance a modern foreign
language had to be found a place in the school curriculum as a
serious time-table subject, it was considered natural, right and
proper that it should be taught along these patterned lines that
had proved their worth' (1957:8).

Of course, as modern educational psychology has discovered,
a double fallacy lies in the traditional belief about the formative
value of Latin as such and of the grammatical method as a means
of mental training especially since the concept of 'transfer of
training' is better understood. Latin has no unique value for

mental discipline. Any well taught subject, for that matter, can train the mental powers of the learner. Nor has it been proved that logical analysis alone can give strength to the reasoning faculty. Any orderly application of the intellective functions to any object of study or action can succeed in exerting a wholesome influence on the mind. It is certainly a lamentable case of mental inertia that these two wrong beliefs have been propagated for over a century without being checked by the majority of language teachers. Perhaps, one may explain this passive sort of tradition by turning to the textbooks used for so many decades by these teachers. They are probably the chief reason for perpetuating an opinion which today appears clearly contrary to common sense and science.

Nineteenth-century textbook compilers were mainly determined to codify the foreign language into frozen rules of morphology and syntax to be explained and eventually memorized. Oral work was reduced to an absolute minimum, while a handful of written exercises, constructed at random, came as a sort of appendix to the rules. Of the many books published during this period, those by Seidenstücker and Plötz were perhaps the most typical and, at least from our point of view, the most baneful, since such compilations became the model for innumerable language textbooks during the nineteenth and first half of the twentieth century.

Johann Heinrich Seidenstücker and Karl Plötz

The first author, Johann Heinrich Seidenstücker (1785-1817), intended, laudably, to offer only very simple material to the students. But he had an erroneous notion of simplicity. In his Elementarbuch zur Erlernung der französischen Sprache (1811), he reduced the material to disconnected sentences to illustrate specific rules. He divided his text carefully into two parts, one giving the rules and necessary paradigms, the other giving French sentences for translation into German and German sentences for translation into French. The immediate aim was for the student to apply the given rules by means of appropriate exercises. Seidenstücker was closely imitated by Karl Plötz (1819-81) who dominated the schools of Germany even after his death. In his textbooks, divided into the two parts described above, the sole form of instruction was mechanical translation. Typical sentences were: 'Thou hast a book. The house is beautiful. He has a kind dog. We have a bread [sic]. The door is black. He has a book and a dog. The horse of the father was kind,' etc.

The manuals prepared by Seidenstücker and Plötz had all the
material that was needed for a thorough drilling in the niceties
of grammar and written French, but no pupil in these classes
would ever have been able to converse with or understand a
Frenchman.

In sum, it was 'a barren waste of insipid sentence translation',
as Bahlsen put it. 'Committing words to memory, translating
sentences, drilling irregular verbs, later memorizing, repeating, and applying grammatical rules with their exceptions—that
was and remained our main occupation; for not until the last
years of the higher schools with the nine-year curriculum did
French reading come to anything like prominence, and that was
the time when free compositions in the foreign language were to
be written' (Bahlsen 1905: 10).

Bahlsen is referring to his own painful experience. He had
been a student of Plötz. He describes a situation still common
today: having to write a letter or to speak in the foreign language
would raise before his mind 'a veritable forest of paragraphs'
and 'an impenetrable thicket of grammatical rules'.

Johann Franz Ahn and H. S. Ollendorf

The same defects can be found in other authors of the same
time, such as Johann Franz Ahn (Französischer Lehrgang, 1834)
and H. S. Ollendorf (Methode, eine Sprache in sechs Monaten
lesen, schreiben und sprechen zu lernen, 1783) (Bahlsen 1905: 10).
The main fault with the Ahn and Ollendorf method was the principle of constructing artificial sentences in order to illustrate a
rule. 'The result', as H. Sweet later remarked, 'is to exclude
the really natural and idiomatic combinations, which cannot be
formed a priori, and to produce insipid, colourless combinations,
which do not stamp themselves on the memory, many of which,
indeed, could hardly occur in real life, such as

> The cat of my aunt is more treacherous than the dog of
> your uncle.
> We speak about your cousin, and your cousin Amelia is
> loved by her uncle and her aunt.
> My sons have bought the mirrors of the duke.
> Horses are taller than tigers.

At one school where I learnt—or rather made a pretence of
learning—Greek on this system, the master used to reconstruct

the materials of the exercises given in our book into new and
strange combinations, till at last, with a faint smile on his
ascetic countenance, he evolved the following sentence, which I
remembered long after I had forgotten all the rest of my Greek—
The philosopher pulled the lower jaw of the hen. The results of
this method have been well parodied by Burnand in his New Sand-
ford and Merton, thus: The merchant is swimming with (avec)
the gardener's son, but the Dutchman has the fine gun' (Sweet
1964: 72-3). [1]

This way of teaching foreign languages became the standard
method during the first half of the nineteenth century, especially
since the proliferation of textbooks modeled on the Plötz outline
placed ready-made tools in the hands of many unskilled teachers.

Henry Wadsworth Longfellow

Fortunately, there were some exceptions to the invading and
deviating trend in the first half of the nineteenth century. In
both Europe and America a few great teachers felt that the right
direction still lay in the natural approach, and they continued to
teach languages in a living manner. One of these great educators
who took the task of modern language teaching seriously was the
American poet, Longfellow (1807-82). It may be worthwhile
quoting a page from a beautifully written article by James Geddes,
who effectively commemorated Longfellow's unique contribution
to the field of modern language teaching. 'It was on the second
of September 1830—a little more than 102 years ago—that Henry
Wadsworth Longfellow delivered his inaugural address in Bowdoin
College upon assuming his duties in the Professorship of the
Modern Languages, to which position the trustees five years
previous had invited him informally after a formal note to establish this chair. In order the better to equip himself for this appointment, Longfellow went to Europe where he spent three years
and a half in travel and study in England and in the principal
European countries ... That Longfellow began his distinguished
career by teaching modern languages has been so overshadowed
by his poetical output throughout his life that his pedagogical
production which followed upon assuming his duties of Professor
of Modern Languages is practically unknown to the average reader.
Finding the elementary treatises of the day poorly adapted to his
course, he prepared no less than seven different textbooks. The
fact that Longfellow brought out seven textbooks between 1830 and
1835 is in itself proof of his seriousness of purpose to teach

French, Italian and Spanish to the best of his ability. Some of
these books were used for many years, a proof of their pedagogical worth and usefulness. They are all small books which, for
beginners, Longfellow preferred to those treating the foreign
languages in extenso' (Geddes 1933: 26).[2] Longfellow treated
languages as living languages, and therefore taught them as
spoken idioms.

George Ticknor

Another great American scholar, George Ticknor (1791-1871),
deserves mention here. He was an example of the best in American culture in contact with European leaders, one of the first
American scholars with an international reputation in the modern
humanities, the first great Hispanist in the United States, a revo-
lutionary educator, and a brilliant teacher of modern languages.
Ticknor's acceptance in 1816 of the newly established Smith
Professorship of the French and Spanish Languages and Litera-
tures at Harvard induced him to spend much time in France,
Spain, Portugal, and Italy. In 1819, after much preparatory
work, he was ready to start his active career. On the scholarly
side, his monumental History of Spanish Literature (1849) can be
considered his masterpiece. On the practical teaching side, we
may be interested in and astonished by his theories of instruction
in the modern foreign languages, which were expressed in his
Lecture on the Best Methods of Teaching the Living Languages
(1833), delivered in 1832. Here sound theory and enlightened
experience go hand in hand. His main ideas can be summed up
briefly as follows:

(1) The primary characteristic of languages is their 'living'
aspect. Ticknor's very first sentence in the lecture is a confes-
sion of faith: 'The most important characteristic of a living language—the attribute in which resides its essential power and
value—is, that it is a spoken one ...'

(2) Therefore, the easiest and best way to acquire a language
is to 'reside where it is constantly spoken', and where it should
be 'the minister to their hourly wants, and the medium of their
constant intercourse'; but since this is not possible for all students, the teachers must, 'while still endeavoring to teach it as
a living and spoken language ... resort to means somewhat more
artificial and indirect'—'the best method within our power at
home'.

(3) 'There is no one mode of teaching languages' applicable 'to persons of all the different ages and different degrees of preparation who present themselves to be taught'. The method must be adapted to individual differences.

(4) Teaching techniques must also be adjusted to different age levels. Ticknor does not agree with those who would have all learners follow the natural way, that is, as a child learns his mother tongue, because 'it is plain', he says, 'that a method adapted to children seven or eight years old would be altogether unsuited to persons in the maturity of their faculties'. Therefore, the method should differ according to the various age levels; and while the oral approach and the inductive teaching of grammar may be advisable for younger learners, the mature students will, he says, 'choose to learn by the analysis of particulars from generals, rather than by the induction of generals from particulars'.

In his sense of balance and his courageous affirmation of progressive principles Ticknor closely approaches current trends in modern language methodology. 'His ideas on the teaching of modern languages, especially, are amazingly in accord with the views of many teachers of the present day' (Newmark 1948: 23).

Practical pioneers

While practice in teaching foreign languages was drifting among the vagaries of formalized grammar and only a few great teachers managed to keep the main principles of sound tradition from total shipwreck, reform was slowly but surely getting under way. The reasserting of a more natural approach was not only the result of loyalty to a long-standing tradition that dated back to ancient civilizations and had been consciously affirmed especially during the seventeenth and eighteenth centuries. It was more particularly the emergence of new ideas within the ranks of such newly born sciences as linguistics and psychology. Representative of the soundest portion of this educational heritage are such teachers as Heness, Marcel, Sauveur, and Gouin. On the linguistic side, Viëtor could be considered as the pioneer of a more scientific reform that arose toward the end of the nineteenth century.

Gottlieb Heness and L. Sauveur

The idea of the 'natural method' as opposed to the grammar-centered procedures introduced by Ahn, Ollendorf, and Plötz

was strongly shared by Gottlieb Heness. Heness started a small
private school of modern languages at New Haven in 1866. His
viewpoint was embodied in his text Leitfaden für den Unterricht
in der deutschen Sprache (1867). Heness was soon joined by another capable teacher, L. Sauveur, the author of Causeries avec
mes élèves and Petites Causeries. They founded a school in
Cambridge, Mass., opened summer schools of modern languages,
counting many outstanding personalities like Eliot, Longfellow,
and Gilman among their students. As Bagster-Collins states:
'These summer schools were largely attended by modern language teachers, who were undoubtedly stimulated to try out in
their classes at least some of the ideas they had gathered during
the five weeks' intensive work' (1930:1).

Claude Marcel

The natural method as practiced by Heness, however, may
have lacked the systematic character demanded by effective teaching. To bring system and order into natural disorder was the aim
of another great pioneer, Claude Marcel, who published his fas-
cinating book, The Study of Languages Brought Back to Its True
Principles, or the Art of Thinking in a Foreign Language, in
1867.[3] The title was a very modern statement of purpose psychologically speaking. Mastering a language was thought to consist not simply in the ability to manipulate forms, but more
radically in the ability to 'think' also in the foreign language
(what today we may call 'coordinate bilingualism'). However,
the systematic character of Marcel's method depended mainly on
a restriction of scope by concentrating primarily on reading.
The essential steps in the 'Marcel method' are the following:
(1) The student's ear is trained by listening to the teacher reading
extensively in the foreign language. (2) The student takes over
by trying to read first simple, and, if possible, familiar material, followed by more and more difficult discourse as he pro-
gresses. (3) Speaking is then practiced on the texts previously
read. (4) Writing is considered the least important ability.
Marcel avoids formal training in grammar or translation. Reading makes up most of the instruction, and grammar does not
seem to help in improving reading comprehension. Dictionaries
also are avoided as they would hamper extensive reading. Marcel
believed that 'twenty-five or thirty volumes at least should be read
to secure the complete acquisition of the art of reading' (1867:54).
He quotes Benjamin Franklin's wise counsel: 'If a book be worth

reading once, it should be read twice'. Then Marcel goes on to say: 'If, at an advanced stage, it is not worth reading twice, it ought not to be read at all ... Productions of sterling worth afford new pleasures, and unfold new beauties at each successive reading; whilst those of inferior character scarcely bear a second perusal; they exhibit more imperfections, according as they are more frequently or attentively read' (1867:64 ff.). It can be easily understood how much Marcel's approach influenced the 'reading method' around 1920.

François Gouin

Heness, Marcel, and Sauveur were European teachers who had left Europe (where Plötz was wielding a dominant influence) and had emigrated to the United States to find a more favorable educational climate. But another European was to exert a large influence in Europe and America. In 1880 the Frenchman, François Gouin, produced his L'art d'enseigner et d'étudier les langues,[4] a work that was at the time completely neglected in France (the author had to have it printed at his own expense), but was a great success in Germany. It took England and America by storm and proved a happy source of inspiration for the later work of the 'direct-methodists'. In his book Gouin tells of his fruitless attempts at learning German by some of the various grammatical methods then in vogue and how one day his own son inspired him with the idea that was to become the basis of his method. The boy had been taken on a visit to a corn mill and came home marveling at all the wonders he had seen. He wanted to have his own mill, and would not rest until his mother had made him some little sacks (to be filled with sand for flour), his uncle had made him a miniature mill, and a stream in the garden had been harnessed to make a waterfall and a mill-race. This is Gouin's own description:

When the mill was definitely mounted and set agoing, the little miller filled his sacks, loaded them on his shoulders with a simulated effort accompanied with a grimace; then bent and grunting beneath the weight, carried his grain to the mill, shot it out and ground it, so reproducing the scene of the real mill—not as he had seen it, but as he had afterwards 'conceived' it to himself, as he had 'generalized' it.

Whilst doing all this, he expressed all his acts aloud, dwelling most particularly upon one word—and this word was the verb, always the verb. The other terms came and tumbled about as they might. Ten times the sack was emptied, refilled, carried to the mill, and its contents ground in imagination.

It was during the course of this operation, carried out again and again without ceasing, 'repeated aloud', that a flash of light suddenly shot across my mind, and I exclaimed softly to myself, 'I have found it! Now I understand!' And following with a fresh interest this precious operation by means of which I had caught a glimpse of the secret so long sought after, I caught sight of a fresh art, that of learning a language. Testing at leisure the truth of my first intuition, and finding it conform more and more to reality, I wandered about repeating to myself the words of the poet, 'Je vois, j'entends, je sais' (Swan and Betis 1892: 129).

Gouin conceived the idea of developing this logical sequence of simple events for school use, known as the 'Gouin Series'. His class procedure was: (1) The teacher explains in the native language the general content of the scene or topic. (2) He enacts the events, describing in the foreign language what he is doing. (3) The single acts are then divided, and again enacted. (4) All this is done first orally, then in writing. There are from eighteen to thirty sentences in a selection. Fifty selections constitute one series. Several series combine to form one general series, and there are five of these: the home, man in society, life in nature, science, and occupations. Each of the headings is subdivided. Thus, the home subdivides into dress, water, fire, heating, the backyard; the stables, the kitchen, the garden, and meetings with people in the locality; man's place in society is subdivided into the school, the church, military service, games, festivals, and illness; occupations include those of the tailor, the shoemaker, the hat manufacturer, the carpenter, the cabinet-maker, the locksmith, the mason; under science are considered the elements and the forces of nature, minerals, plants, animals (wild and domestic), rodents, birds, fishes, amphibians, reptiles, insects; and, finally, life in nature gives rise to a subseries—the shepherd, the hunter, the fisherman, the harvester, the ploughman, the carpenter, the baker, fields, meadows, vineyards, gardens, forests and agricultural crafts. Thus 50,000 sentences and 8,000 words are presented in the whole system. It is an elaborate and ambitious scheme. The following example shows how Gouin put his method into practice:

> We will suppose the occasion to be a lesson in French, beginning with the exercise by which we generally initiate pupils into our method: 'I open the door of the classroom.' First of all I briefly announce this aim, and present it as such. Then I set forth in the native tongue of the children the successive means by which this end can be attained, to wit:

I walk towards the door	I walk
I draw near to the door	I draw near
I draw nearer and nearer	I draw nearer
I get to the door	I get to
I stop at the door	I stop
I stretch out my arm	I stretch out
I take hole of the handle	I take hold
I turn the handle	I turn
I open the door	I open
I pull the door	I pull
The door moves	moves
The door turns on its hinges	turns
The door turns and turns	turns
I open the door wide	I open
I let go the handle	let go

The end proposed is attained, my volition is realized; I stop. My exercise is dictated and written not upon the paper, but in the ears; and by way of the ears it has penetrated the mind.

One of the pupils, the weakest or the most distracted, should now go through this analysis again in English, and the whole class should be invited to imagine clearly to themselves not only the end, but the successive means by which it can be attained.

This done, and when the whole class have 'thought' the exercise, the teacher once more takes the phrase in English, detaches the verb—I walk, and thereupon throws the French verb—marche, upon which he emphasises by repeating it several times over, slowly—marche, marche, marche.

He then calls for the second sentence ... etc. etc.
(1892:129-30).

An original example taken from Gouin's Erstes Übungsbuch
für das Deutsche would be the following:

Der Hund sucht. Er sucht und sucht. Er wittert eine
Kette Rebhühner. Er tut eine Kette Rebhühner auf. Er
steht. Er geht auf den Befehl des Jägers vor. Die
Rebhühner bemerken (sehen) den Hund. Sie fürchten sich
vor dem Hunde. Sie fliegen auf. Sie fliegen davon. Der
Jäger sieht die Kette Hühner davonfliegen. Er ergreift
sein Gewehr. Er legt an (führt das Gewehr zur Schulter).
Er zielt und zielt. Er drückt ab. Der Schusz geht los.
Die Ladung trifft ein Huhn. Das Huhn fällt zur Erde
(Kron 1895: 22 ff.)

The new element that Gouin brought into the teaching of modern languages was intense activity through dramatization of the
sentences to be drilled. Language was no longer considered a
construct of isolated pieces, something abstract to be anatomized
and then pieced together again. 'Language is behavior', Gouin
could say today. Therefore, association, mimicry, memorization constituted the pivotal activities of language learning.
Furthermore, his ingenious classification of activities into what
a modern educator, Ovide Decroly, later called 'centers of interest' was meeting not only the child's need for activity, but also
its need for concrete and familiar experiences. A third positive
aspect to be found in Gouin's method is certainly represented by
his use of complete sentences anchored in true-to-life situations
instead of fragments of speech taken out of living context.
    But, on the other hand, several methodological weaknesses
tend to jeopardize the effectiveness of Gouin's approach. His
opposition to phonetics, reading, and written exercises and his
recommendation of a large vocabulary, not graded by difficulty
or frequency, are both weaknesses in light of modern applied
linguistics. Furthermore, unlike Comenius, Pestalozzi, and most
modern teachers, Gouin distrusted Realien and pictorial repre-
sentation and placed his faith instead in a vague intuitive awareness. Finally, the exaggerated analysis of speech and behavior
into 'micro-segments' and the excessive use of translation (especially in the early stages) endanger the positive effects of Gouin's
main procedures.

Gouin did, however, inaugurate a new era in language teaching by introducing a 'systematic psychological approach'.

The practical innovations of such talented teachers as Heness, Sauveur, Marcel, and Gouin did not impress the public until science stepped in to strengthen the appeal of the new methodology. In fact, the 'reform movement' came to be officially recognized only when noted linguists became enthusiastic spokesmen for the advancing trend. It was especially the new science of phonetics, 'the science of speech sounds and the art of pronunciation', as it was called by Henry Sweet, that supplied the first scientific basis for the reformed methodology. Alexander John Ellis had published his Essentials of Phonetics (1848), E. Brücke his Grundzüge der Physiologie und der Systematik der Sprachlaute (1856), Alexander Bell his Visible Speech (1867) and his Sounds and their Relations (1882). The new science of linguistics was basically reduced to descriptive phonetics; and it seemed that this science of sounds could promise intriguing new developments in the teaching of modern languages. Furthermore, deep changes in the fundamental structure of European society and in the whole economic outlook were creating new demands upon culture and school education. Germany and England had become industrial nations and strong colonial powers. Colonial exploitation and commercial enterprise depended not only on industrial undertakings, but also on adequate foreign language training. The problems of that transitional period were similar to the ones confronting our post-World War II generation.

Wilhelm Viëtor

In sum, the impact on language teaching came from two fronts, the economic and the scientific. The phoneticians—Henry Sweet, Sievers, Trautmann, Helmholtz, Passy, Rambeau, Klinghardt, and others—set themselves untiringly to develop this new science, so much so that it came to be considered an indispensable help in any language course. Archibald Sayce applied phonetics to the problems of language teaching. Wilhelm Viëtor (1850-1918) issued a pamphlet entitled Der Sprachunterricht musz umkehren: ein Beitrag zur Überburdungsfrage (1882), over the bellicose signature of Quousque tandem ('How much longer?', the first words of Cicero's First Oration against Catiline).[5] 'With withering sarcasm he denounced all the supporters of the Plötz method and insisted that the spoken language become the basis of instruction; it is through the ear that the child learns its mother tongue, it is through the ear that a more mature person must begin the study of a foreign language. The teacher, therefore, must have a firm grasp of phonetics; and he must have resided long enough in the foreign country to have mastered and to be able to teach an exact pronunciation. Again, a language is not made up of isolated words, but of word-groups, of 'speech-patterns', of sentences that mean something. No more lists of words, therefore, to be learned laboriously by heart; no more meaningless snippets of sentences, void of all interest and real meaning; no more grammatical paradigms. Grammar is to be learned inductively, and translation, a most difficult exercise, is not to be used for the acquisition of new vocabulary, but as an art that requires considerable maturity of knowledge of the foreign tongue before it can profitably be indulged' (Mallinson 1957: 14-15).[6] Viëtor's appeal was heard all over Europe and also in America, especially after he started a review, Die neuren Sprachen, that popularized the new approach.

Walter Ripman

In Great Britain, one of Viëtor's disciples made his voice heard. He was Walter Ripman, who belonged to a small band of English pioneers who had attended the first modern-language summer course at Marburg after the publication of Viëtor's pamphlet. He came away a convinced supporter and in 1899 published his translation and adaptation of Viëtor's Kleine Phonetik (Elements of Phonetics)—a book that established itself as a classic in England.

In the same period, a Swiss by the name of Alge in 1887 started to use colored wall pictures, introduced in 1885 by a Viennese, Holzel, to the teaching of modern languages. Thus the now famous wall pictures of the seasons, of trades and occupations, and of village and town life, came into existence. Ripman, in collaboration with Alge, wrote his First French Book (1898). This was the beginning of a long collaboration between Ripman and his publishers, J. M. Dent & Sons, for whom he remained the general modern language editor until his death in 1947.

The reform movement was encouraged by conferences held at Vienna in 1898 and at Leipzig in 1900. Gradually textbooks took on a different pattern. Phonetic instruction loomed large in the earlier chapters. The mother tongue was entirely banished. Vocabulary and grammatical forms were to be assimilated inductively or intuitively (by mime or gesture, by pictures, drawings, illustrations, by definition in terms of the words and expressions already mastered, or from context). The reading passages consisted mainly of simple modern prose designed to introduce the pupil to an understanding of the life and customs of the foreign people and to their history and geography. Speech first, reading second, writing last of all became the established order in the course of elementary instruction. Translation into either language was forbidden.

The claims of the reformers were not, however, accepted peacefully. Reactions on the part of teachers and scholars arose not only because of irrational attachment to old practices, but also because of the initial chaos caused by the unsystematic and rigid application of the new precepts to differing teaching situations and by enthusiastic but unprepared novice teachers. Lack of clear objectives and flexibility was frequently the cause of students flunking examinations or failing to get a firm grasp of the language they were supposed to be studying. Consequently, teachers followed one of two courses: some reverted to the old grammar-grind tactics and to the Plötz approach; others tried some sort of compromise between the oral approach and the use of reading and grammar. It was a 'tamed' direct method. A final summing up of the controversy over the original direct method appeared in 1909. It read:

The Reform has fulfilled its mission. It has laid the ghosts of the grammatical method, which made a fetish of the study of grammar with excessive attention to translation from and into the foreign language. Reading formerly served chiefly as a handmaiden to grammar, and was too exclusively limited to historical-literary works. Speaking ability was kept in the background and correct pronunciation was neglected. Such an antiquated method of teaching is now once and for all impossible. But what the grammatical method neglected, practical and correct use of the spoken language, the reform method has pushed to extremes. In making mastery of the spoken language the chief objective, the nature and function of secondary schools was overlooked, because such an objective under normal conditions of mass instruction is only attainable in a modest degree. The reform method requires not only a teacher who possesses a perfect mastery of the foreign language, but makes such claims on his nervous and physical energy as to entail premature exhaustion.

Average pupils, not to mention weaker ones, do not justify the demands made by the oral use of the language;
they soon weary, are overburdened and revolt. Early
adherents of the new method, after their enthusiasm has
been dashed by stern realities, have gradually broken
away (cited by Buchanan and MacPhee 1928: 19 ff.).[7]

NOTES

[1] Manufacturing the language that was intended to be learned,
but as a work of the pupil himself and not of the teacher, was a
process that had been already introduced by Johann Valentin
Meidinger (1756-1820), and was therefore appropriately called
Meidingerei by Wilhelm Viëtor. Meidinger published in 1783 a
book with the alluring title: Praktische französische Grammatik,
wodurch man diese Sprache auf eine ganz neue und sehr leichte
Art in kurzer Zeit erlernen kann. The textbook works from the
grammatical rule to translation into the foreign language with the
aid of footnotes so that new foreign sentences can be concocted
by the pupil himself.
[2] Cf. also Longfellow, Samuel (1886:175-6).
[3] Cf. also C. Marcel (1853).
[4] The 1880 edition was translated by Howard Swan and Victor
Betis (1892). We quote from this edition.
[5] Viëtor's pamphlet appeared later in an enlarged and annotated edition: Leipzig, 1905.
[6] Other important works by Viëtor were Elemente der
Phonetik des deutschen, englischen und französischen (1884);
Phonetische Studien (1887/93).
[7] Breymann and Steinmuller (1895-1909) collected, summarized and evaluated a large number of books and articles that appeared during the controversial years. Cf. also Escher (1919).

4

HENRY SWEET

The partial failure of the 'natural method' (later named the 'direct method' by the methodologists at the end of the nineteenth and beginning of the twentieth century) called for a more scientific foundation and a few practical adjustments. Credit for further refinement of the direct method goes to a series of teachers and scholars who were scientifically minded and at the same time deeply concerned with the future of modern language teaching. From this group of dedicated scholars three outstanding leaders can be singled out: Henry Sweet, Otto Jespersen, and Harold E. Palmer.[1]

Sweet's life and orientation

Henry Sweet (1845-1912), a celebrated English philologist, received his education in England and in Heidelberg, Germany. He knew many languages, both ancient and modern—Sanskrit, Latin, Greek, Old Irish, Welsh, French, German, Finnish, Arabic, Chinese, Italian, and others. He was such an authority on phonetics that a readership in phonetics was created especially for him by the University of Oxford in 1901. But he also felt the need of applying the new science of linguistics, especially phonetics, to practical teaching in order to save modern language teaching from floundering. His keen interest in methodology is attested by the nature of the majority of his works, as can be seen from the following: Primer of Phonetics (1890), Elementarbuch des gesprochenen Englisch (1891), Anglo-Saxon Primer (1893), Primer of Spoken English (1895), First Steps in Anglo-Saxon (1897), The Practical Study of Languages (1899), The History of Language (1900), A New

English Grammar (after 1900?), Collected Papers of Henry Sweet
edited by H. C. Wyld (1913).

Sweet's methodological orientation can be defined on the basis
of the following characteristics.

(1) He was first of all convinced that the practical study of
languages was in no way less scientific than the theoretical. A
study of modern languages could become scientific by accepting
as its basis what he called 'living philology', by which he meant
an approach consisting of some sort of descriptive linguistics,
especially phonetics, and psychology.

(2) The starting point of his method was to be a set of 'general
principles' derived from the analysis of language in general, followed by 'special principles' concerning each particular language.
Analysis of each language is an indispensable prerequisite for a
good method. This explains why older methods, like those advocated by Ollendorff, Ahn, and others, had failed. These methods,
says Sweet, 'are failures because they are based on an insuffi-
cient knowledge of the science of language, and because they are
one-sided ... A good method must, before all, be comprehensive
and eclectic. It must be based on a thorough knowledge of the
science of language—phonetics, sound-notation, the grammatical
structure of a variety of representative languages, and linguistic
problems generally. In utilizing this knowledge it must be constantly guided by the psychological laws on which memory and the
association of ideas depend' (1964, p. 3).

(3) In Sweet's day the scientific study of language was mainly
focused on the study of speech sounds. This explains his primary
emphasis. 'The main axiom of living philology, he says, is that
all study of language must be based on phonetics' (1964:4).

(4) 'The second main axiom of living philology is that all study
of language, whether theoretical or practical, ought to be based
on the spoken language' (1964:49). Against some outdated gram-
marians, Sweet was strong in maintaining that the spoken language
is the source of the written language, that 'the real life of language is better seen in dialects and colloquial forms of speech
than in highly developed literary languages, such as Greek, Latin,
and Sanskrit' (1964:50). Moreover, practical considerations,
such as the functional character of spoken grammar and vocabulary
in contrast to the complication of literary forms, would suggest
the necessity, or at least the utility, of emphasizing the spoken
language, especially at the beginning. By starting from the spoken
language we have less to learn, and we learn it accurately. Everything therefore points to the conclusion that in learning foreign

languages we should follow the natural order in which we learn
our own language: that is, 'that we should begin with learning the
spoken language thoroughly, and then go on to the literary language' (1964:51).[2]

(5) Sweet is modern not only for his emphasis on the spoken
language, but also for his awareness of the problem of cross-
linguistic contrasts, which contemporary 'contrastive linguistics'
has also stressed. Besides some external difficulties due to the
circumstances under which a language is learned, 'there is another class of difficulties', Sweet observes, 'which may be regarded as partly external, partly internal—those which depend on
the relations of the foreign language to the learner's native language, especially as regards similarity in vocabulary and structure' (1964:53-4). In other words, the contrast may be greater
precisely where there appear to be similarities (deceitful similarities or false cognates). The real difficulty, Sweet believes,
is in learning the vocabulary. 'We can master enough of the
grammar of any language for reading purposes within a definite
period—generally less than six months—but we cannot do the
same with the vocabulary unless it is already partially familiar
to us ... ' (1964:64-5). Consequently, effective teaching demands
the identification of the contrasts between the first and the second
language in order to foresee and eliminate problems of interference.

It is evident that Sweet conceived of scientific methodology as
supported by linguistic and psychological postulates, but he
leaned heavily toward linguistics, as the following analysis of his
principles will prove.

General principles

The general principles of method, found in chapter nine, are
directly derived from linguistics. The objective study of languages reveals that each language has its own peculiar constructions, idioms, and meanings, and therefore must be studied as it
is, not as some extraneous paradigm would tend to show it.
Chinese, for example, cannot be interpreted on the basis of Latin
grammar.

Furthermore, 'it is important to realize clearly the fact that
language is partly rational, partly irrational and arbitrary'
(1964:69). Language is usually more rational or systematic in
the grammar and less so in the vocabulary. But both in the
vocabulary and in the grammar there are frequent irrational

combinations, that is, constructions or forms which result from arbitrariness and do not follow a rigid rule. 'One result of language being partly rational, partly irrational, is that some of its phenomena can be brought under general rules, some cannot ... This constitutes the whole distinction between grammar and dictionary. Grammar, like all other sciences, deals with what can be brought under general laws, and relegates all the other phenomena of language to that collection of isolated facts which we call dictionary' (1964:73).

From the point of view of method, one can overstress the separation of grammar and dictionary and concentrate on studying them separately, or, as with the direct-methodists, merge grammar and dictionary into natural communicative situations. Sweet criticizes the pure 'natural method' both on linguistic and psychological grounds. 'These enthusiasts', he says, 'forget that the process of learning one's native language is carried on under peculiarly favourable circumstances, which cannot be even approximately reproduced in the later study of foreign languages' (1964:74). 'The fundamental objection, then, to the natural method is that it puts the adult into the position of an infant, which he is no longer capable of utilizing, and, at the same time, does not allow him to make use of his own special advantages. These advantages are ... the power of analysis and generalization—in short, the power of using a grammar and dictionary' (1964:75).

Sweet felt that the best of the old methods should be combined with the best of the new. Systematic study of grammar, although retained, has to be made more practical, by repeated drill on living language material. Meaningful spoken sentences are to become the direct material for assimilation by the student. Understanding how the language works is only part of the task. The rest belongs to direct absorption. In fact, since languages are only partly rational, 'their acquisition must be, to a great extent at least, a mechanical process' (1964:79). In sum, as Sweet states in his Preface, 'my attitude towards the traditional methods is, as will be seen, a mean between unyielding conservatism on the one hand and reckless radicalism on the other. There are some fundamental principles on which I insist, whether they are popular or not, such as basing all study of language on phonetics, and starting from the spoken rather than the literary language. But, on the other hand, the reader will find that while I agree with the Continental reformers in condemning the practice of exercise-writing and the use of a priori methods such as Ahn's, I refuse to join with them in their condemnation of translation and the use of grammar' (1964:vii-viii). Therefore, what Sweet means by 'rational method' does not exclude direct practice with authentic language materials, but actually demands it.

Special principles

Sweet's methodological approach can best be seen from the articulation of the following 'special principles' of sound scientific method of language teaching (1964:ch.10).

(1) 'The psychological foundation of the practical study of languages is the great law of association ... The whole process of learning a language is one of forming associations. When we learn our own language, we associate words and sentences with thoughts, ideas, actions, events' (1964:102). Sweet was obviously drawing his psychological principles from a common-sense psychology of language learning and, possibly, from the scientific psychology of his day, which was largely associationistic. This is particularly evident from the detailed rules which he listed as deriving from association theory: (a) 'Present the most frequent and necessary elements first.' (b) 'Present like and like together.' (c) 'Contrast like with unlike till all sense of effort in the transition ceases.' (d) 'Let the associations be as definite as possible.' (e) 'Let the associations be direct and concrete, not indirect and abstract.' (f) 'Avoid conflicting associations (cross-associations)'(1964:104-8). Even today none of these rules could be reasonably rejected.

(2) 'Repetition is essential both for forming associations and retaining them in the memory' (1964:109). However, repetition work should not be carried to the point of tiring out the student. The teacher should work with a limited vocabulary. And 'learning by heart should not be attempted till the piece has been thoroughly studied from all sides' (1964:110).

(3) 'Memory depends also on attention, and this partly on the interest taken in the subject.' Sweet, however, is clear in rejecting the cultivation of superficial interests which would only divert the learner from the real task. 'If the learner is interested in the language itself, that is enough' (1964:111-2).

(4) Language texts, grammar, and dictionary should be well related. 'The beginner's grammar ought to deal only with the inflections and constructions which actually occur in the texts he is reading, and the dictionary—if a dictionary is used at all— ought to take the form of a special glossary to those texts'

(1964:114). Sweet advocates some sort of 'inductive method' which he is careful to distinguish from the exaggerations of the so-called 'inventional methods'. The latter, he thought, would have the pupils deduce all the rules of grammar from the texts by patient, and at times frustrating, discovery. The former presupposes that the teacher has already acquainted the pupils with some characteristic examples of a definite grammatical category as a guide to finding other typical examples and to clas- sifying them into paradigms. The 'inductive method' consists mainly in collecting paradigmatic material that is intuitively sensed to belong to common grammatical classes, as a prepara- tion for the formal study of grammar (1964:115 ff.).

(5) Grammar is to be taught formally only after it has been absorbed intuitively from the texts. It is at this point that Sweet, while distinguishing himself from the outdated formal grammatical approach, appears to be very much in line with modern linguists. He maintains, first of all, that 'the more unfamiliar the language, the greater the amount of grammatical analysis required, and the more elaborate and detailed it must be' (1964:96). Thus there is no question of abolishing grammar. Certain criteria in teaching grammar must, however, be kept in mind. 'From a practical, as well as a scientific, point of view, the sentence is the unit of language, not the word ... From the point of view of the practical study of language the synthetic method implies that the analysis of the language is not carried further than, at the most, cutting it up into sentences, which are grasped and learnt as wholes' (1964:97). 'Syntax is the most important part of the grammar, and ... it re- quires a much fuller and more detailed treatment than the acci- dence' (1964:95). Sweet is much in agreement with modern struc- tural and functional views which emphasize the study of linguistic wholes or 'patterns'. He rejects, accordingly, the memorization of lists of words, of paradigms, and of detached sentences without relation to context. His strong opposition to the Ollendorff sys- tem stems from these convictions (1964:101 ff.). [3]

(6) Finally, Sweet outlines the stages of his 'progressive method' (1964:117 ff.).

The first stage, the 'mechanical' stage, begins with a thorough mastery of the pronunciation of the language. 'Every sentence must be practised till it runs glibly off the tongue without effort or hesitation' (1964:117). Many irregularities should be learned in this stage, as the phonetic exercises will include some of the most necessary and frequent elements of the grammar and vocabulary.

The 'grammatical' stage will follow as soon as the student has acquired a thorough mastery of the pronunciation and enough material for grammatical study. 'In this stage the texts will be so chosen as to embody the different grammatical categories in progressive order of difficulty as far as is compatible with employing genuine texts which reproduce the actual language' (1964: 119). Of course, the study of grammar will be continued during all the following stages.

The third stage is the 'idiomatic and lexical'. Here the idioms will be learned systematically, 'partly from reading idiomatic texts, partly from a phraseology in which the idioms will be classed under psychological categories'. The result is 'a thorough command of a limited number of words and phrases and idioms expressing the most necessary ideas' (1964:120).

In the 'literary' stage texts from literature, which are more varied in form and more difficult in structure, are presented, since the mastery of grammar and vocabulary acquired so far enables the student to choose his texts with greater freedom and with less subordination of matter to form.

The fifth stage, the 'archaic', involves moving from contemporary literature to older forms of the same language, going either from the past to the present or from the present to the past. Of course, this stage can come only at the end of the process of language instruction, when the student has acquired a thorough mastery of the modern literary language in its most important branches.

Sweet outlined with precision the various procedures that could be used in teaching the foreign language at these different stages. He took issue with those reformers who have rejected the use of translation, at least from the foreign language. He maintained that this 'is at the same time the most obvious and convenient way of explaining its meaning' (1964:198). Of course, as will be seen with other critics of the pure direct method such as Palmer, Jespersen and others, Sweet does not mean to say that seeking for the literal equivalents of foreign isolated items should be accepted as a valid procedure. This word-for-word transfer cannot be considered as genuine translation of the language as a structured system. 'Thinking in the foreign language' will come later as a result of a more direct association between the foreign phrase and its meaning. Obviously, translating into the foreign language will demand a higher stage of mastery than a beginner possesses.

Many other theoretical and even more practical questions are examined in Sweet's book from which the above quotations have been taken. Indeed, no relevant problems of foreign language teaching discussed by today's methodologists escaped his alert mind. The 1964 edition of Sweet's book is quite justified: this treatise is a veritable classic in the history of applied linguistics.

Evaluation of Sweet's contribution

The foregoing observations make it possible to draw a general evaluation of Henry Sweet's contribution to the reform of language teaching methodology.

What strikes the reader of Sweet's publications immediately is his devotion to the cause of scientific progress in teaching foreign languages. His attitude of reasonable cautiousness that keeps him from either yielding to the old practices or blindly accepting the new brand of reformed methodology, is the fruit of genuine scientific spirit. But a closer scrutiny of his ideas shows him to be more 'progressive' than he intends to be in his cautious statements. Most of the old teaching routines are courageously discarded by Sweet because they cannot stand the test of scientific linguistics or psychology. In short, Sweet was the mature representative of 'moderate direct-methodism'.

Sweet's book The Practical Study of Languages can be considered the first comprehensive, systematic treatise on the methodology of foreign-language teaching. Its object was 'to indicate the lines of abstract research and practical work along which the path of progress lies' (1964:vii). Many contemporary methodologists would benefit greatly by going back to the lucid pages written by Sweet.

Again, he had the merit, unique in his day, of seeing the need of a theoretical framework for the elaboration of a sound methodology. This he based on linguistic and psychological principles. The elaboration of a good method involves: (a) the selection of the language to be taught; (b) the limitation of the amount to be taught in any given course; (c) the arrangement of the selected material in terms of the four language skills of understanding speech, speaking, reading, and writing; and (d) the grading of the details of the material at the various levels of pronunciation, grammar, vocabulary, and cultural content.[4] These are the working phases typically followed by contemporary applied linguistics. The same are the phases postulated, more or less explicitly, by Sweet in delineating his methodological itinerary. Therefore, it seems right to consider Henry Sweet as the 'father of applied linguistics' in the modern sense of the phrase.

Certain theoretical emphases, however, which were current in his day, tended to weigh too heavily in his thinking. This may explain why he overstressed somewhat indiscriminately the teaching of theoretical phonetics and the use of phonetic symbols.[5]

Moreover, his choice of the age of ten as the time to begin learning foreign languages was daring for his time, but runs counter to our prevailing convictions and experiences. Finally, his associationistic psychology is truly old-fashioned. But this is a limitation due mainly to his times and does not diminish the outstanding value of Sweet's contribution.

NOTES

[1] Besides Sweet, Jespersen, and Palmer, it is well to remember some of the other scholars and the dates of their principal publications. These include F. Franke (1896), W. H. Widgery (1888), H. Klinghardt (1888 and 1892), H. Breymann (1895), M. Brebner (1898), and P. Passy (1899). O. Jespersen, in the preliminary pages of his book How To Teach a Foreign Language, acknowledges his indebtedness to a longer series of linguists.

[2] Psychologically speaking, separating the spoken language from the literary during the course of study would be a way of avoiding or minimizing cross-associations between the two forms of the language. (Cf. 1964:12 and 51.)

[3] 'One of the great weaknesses of the a priori methods of the Ollendorff type is that they involve the substitution of detached sentences for connected texts.' (p. 100). '... Each detached sentence is regarded as a bag into which is crammed as much grammatical and lexical information as it will hold.' (p. 101).

[4] This distribution by R. Mackin, as is incidentally proposed in his Preface to the 1964 edition of Sweet's book, can be accepted almost unanimously and supplies a fairly good basis for evaluating Sweet's linguistic bias.

[5] Chapter 2 is devoted to an introduction to the study of phonetics; Chapter 3 deals with phonetic notation; Chapter 6 with special techniques of teaching phonetics. Among the other things, Sweet's interest in phonetic notation led him to improve on Ellis' English Glossic and devise his Romic system using ordinary letters supplemented by special types and diacritical marks. The present IPA comes from Sweet's initial system as it was adapted by P. Passy.

5

OTTO JESPERSEN

Among the early scientific reformers of language teaching methodology, Otto Jespersen (1860-1943) must be granted a prominent position. As professor of English at the University of Copenhagen and professor of linguistics at Columbia University, in 1909-10, Jespersen is known mainly for his writings on the English language and general linguistics and hence is better known as a linguist than a teaching methodologist. One little pamphlet on the teaching of foreign languages, however, gained him lasting fame also in the field of applied linguistics. The following list of Jespersen's publications, although not complete, is sufficiently indicative of his interests and contributions.

Textbooks:
Fransk Begynderbog (1901)
Kortfattet engelsk Grammatik (1903)
Engelsk Begynderbog (1902, 1903)
The England and America Reader (1903)

Scientific publications:
Progress in Language (1894)
Fonetik (1897-99)
Lehrbuch der Phonetik (1904)
Sprogundervisning (How to Teach a Foreign Language) (1904 ff.)
Modern English Grammar (1904-47 ff.) (7 vols.)
Growth and Structure of the English Language (1905)
Language, Its Nature, Development, and Origin (1922)
Philosophy of Grammar (1924)

Mankind, Nation and Individual from a Linguistic Point of
   View (1925)
Novial Lexike (vocabulary of the author's international
   language (1930)
Essentials of English Grammar (1933)
A System of Grammar (1933)
Linguistics (1933)
Selected Writings (1960)

Most of the new editions have been published by Allen and
Unwin, London. For more details see Jespersen's autobiography,
En sprogmands levned (Copenhagen, 1938), and T. A. Sebeok
(ed.) Portraits of Linguists 1746-1963, vol. II, Bloomington,
Indiana University Press, 1966, pp. 148-173. In the honorary
volume of 1930 there is a bibliography of Jespersen's works by
C. A. Bodelsen.

General methodological orientation

Jespersen's general orientation in the methodology of foreign
language teaching is not essentially different from Sweet's.
   First, his methodology line is based on a manifold approach:
linguistic, especially phonetic, theory, as well as commonsense
psychology and sound teaching practice. He acknowledges his indebtedness to several linguists and outstanding teachers, refus-
ing to limit his method to a single approach, thus keeping it open
to all the best suggestions that theory and practice might offer.
'If', as he says in one of the introductory pages of his booklet,
'in old Norse mythology, the god Heimdall had nine mothers,
our reform method has at least seven wise fathers' (1947:3). At
the origin of Jespersen's methodology stand 'men who, for other
reasons, may claim a place among the most eminent linguistic
scholars of the last decades (Sweet, Storm, Sievers, Sayce,
Lundell, and others), and the ideas which they have conceived
have been adopted and applied to life with many practical innovations and changes by a large number of educators and schoolmasters (I may mention almost at random Klinghardt, Walter, Kühn,
Dörr, Quiehl, Rossmann, Wendt, Widgery, Western, Brekke);
on the boundary between both groups stand especially Viëtor and
Paul Passy. That shows that it is not with theoretical sophistries
that we have to do; it is not the whim of one man, but the sum of
all the best linguistical and pedagogical ideas of our times, which,
coming from many different sources, have found each other, and

have made a beautiful alliance for the purpose of overturning the old routine' (1947:3-4).

Second, Jespersen starts from the conviction that the teaching of 'living' languages must not be rigid and strictly logical. 'Modern languages ... want to be treated as living, and the method of teaching them must be as elastic and adaptable as life is restless and variable' (1947:4).

Finally, languages are made for communication. Therefore, 'we ought to learn a language through sensible communications; there must be (and this as far as possible from the very first day) a certain connection in the thoughts communicated in the language' (1947:11). This means, first, that language must be studied as a whole, the way it is organized overall, that is in its total structure, and not by a minute analysis of its individual components; second, that language, to be grasped in its living meaningfulness, must be studied in context and in communication situations.[1] If, as Jespersen rightly maintains, the living language is to be the primary object of teaching, then grammar and vocabulary cannot be the aim of language study but must be functionally subordinated to the process of understanding and assimilating the language as a living whole. Logically, selection of grammar and vocabulary according to use and frequency becomes primary for the language teacher and the author of textbooks. 'The beginner has only use for the most everyday words; he ought to have nothing to do with the vocabulary of poetry or even of more elevated prose; like everything superfluous, it is detrimental, because it burdens the memory and hinders perfect familiarity with that which is most necessary' (1947:19-20).

'Language as communication' is therefore the leading criterion both for Sweet and Jespersen in devising an effective method.

Special principles

The 'special principles' of method proposed by the Danish linguist all center upon two concepts: first, what is to be studied is the 'living' language and second, such study must be carried on by 'direct contact' with it.

(1) The living language, however, for Jespersen is not necessarily the spoken conversational language, but the one offered in easy readers as bases of systematic instruction. Good reading selections are to be the foundation for language study, with the requirements that they must: (a) be connected and have a sensible meaning; (b) be interesting, lively, and varied; (c) contain the

most needed material of the language first, especially the mate -
rial of everyday speech; (d) be correct language; (e) pass gradu -
ally from that which is easy to that which is more difficult;
(f) do these things without too much consideration for what is
merely grammatically easy or difficult (1947:23).

(2) By direct contact Jespersen means a sort of immersion of
the pupil in the language. 'The first condition', he says, 'for
good instruction in foreign languages would seem to be to give
the pupil as much as possible to do with and in the foreign lan -
guage; he must be steeped in it, not only get a sprinkling of it
now and then; he must be ducked down in it and get to feel as if
he were in his own element, so that he may at last disport him -
self in it as an able swimmer' (1947:48). Some of his principles
are the logical consequences of his concept of 'direct contact':

(a) If the contact with the living language is to be direct, no
dominant use should be made of translation.[2]

(b) Oral work must dominate, taking the form of memoriza -
tion and repetition of foreign texts already explained and under -
stood (the same view was held by Sweet).

(c) Exercises should be numerous and varied in character.
According to Jespersen, one of the most important exercises is
to transpose a selection which has been read into questions and
answers (1947:100 ff.). A second variety is renarration (still
widely used today in German schools under the name of
Nacherzählung (cf. 1947:105 ff.).

(d) No analytic or formal grammar should be taught per se;
on the contrary, grammar shall be implicitly assimilated through
live practice on grammatical patterns. First, the teacher will
guide the pupils to discover the facts of grammar by pointing them
out or having them pointed out as an appropriate selection is being
read. This he calls 'inventional grammar',[3] a sort of inductive
study of grammar. But above all, grammar must be grasped
globally and functionally. Teaching grammar 'functionally' (the
term is not used by Jespersen, but is used in recent European
didactic publications) means that morphology and syntax should
be presented together. 'The sharp division between accidence
and syntax as we find it in most of our textbooks is, from a
scientific point of view, untenable and impracticable; from a
pedagogical point of view it is unfortunate, because it separates
form and function, which ought to be learned together, just as
well as a word's exterior (its sounds and spelling) and its mean -
ing are learned together' (1947:134).[4] At any rate, 'theoretical
grammar ought not to be taken up too early, and when it is taken

up it is not well to do it in such a way that the pupil is given ready-made paradigms and rules' (1947:127).

(3) Reading as an instructional starting point, however, should not mean exclusion of the spoken language and oral exercise: rather, the contrary is true. Jespersen, like the linguists of his day, believed firmly in phonetics, as he lost no opportunity to state. 'We want to have some phonetics introduced into our schools', he writes, 'because theory has convinced us, and experiment has proved to us, that by means of this science we can, with decidedly greater certainty, and in an essentially easier way, give an absolutely better pronunciation in a much shorter space of time than would be possible without phonetics' (1947:143). Therefore, 'the very first lesson in a foreign language ought to be devoted to initiating the pupils into the world of sounds' (1947: 146).[5] Jespersen's conviction had the vigor of a new idea just discovered and found fruitful. 'The use of phonetics and phonetical transcription in the teaching of modern languages must be considered as one of the most important advances in modern pedagogy, because it ensures both considerable facilitation and an exceedingly large gain in exactness' (1947:176).

Evaluation of Jespersen's contribution

Jespersen's contribution cannot be underestimated. As with Sweet, his teaching method attains a greater maturity and solidity due to a better understanding of the nature of language. It is Jespersen's linguistic sophistication more than his educational common sense that guarantees the validity of his principles.

Besides having scientific foundation, Jespersen's methodology is also adaptable to the practical teaching situation. His small book, issued over half a century ago, can still inspire modern teachers by suggesting down-to-earth devices and procedures for adapting the results of linguistic analyses to the assimilative capacity of even very young learners. His lengthy demonstrations, e.g. on how to teach elementary phonetics, are convincing examples of some of the best procedures of effective teaching.

Jespersen's insistence on the primacy of language as sound and spoken communication is valuable, especially with respect to the beginning phases of language instruction.

With the exception of his slight overemphasis on reading at the very beginning of language study, most of his tenets can be considered valid even today and mark him as among the first in the field now called applied linguistics.

NOTES

[1] Like Sweet, Jespersen stresses at the very beginning the importance of using as language material sensible portions of communicative speech and banters the ridiculous fashion of many books current in his days which would pile up haphazardly words or sentences totally disconnected from each other. 'Disconnected words are but stones for bread', he says; 'one cannot say anything sensible with mere lists of words. Indeed not even disconnected sentences ought to be used, at all events, not in such manner and to such an extent as in most books according to the old method. For there is generally just as little connexion between them as there would be in a newspaper if the same line were read all the way across from column to column' (1947:11). There is essentially one reason for this aberration: grammar is the chief culprit; what matters above all is the drilling of grammatical rules. 'The raison d'être of each sentence lies merely in its value for the grammatical exercises, so that by reading school-books one often gets the impression that Frenchmen must be strictly systematical beings, who one day speak merely in futures, another day in passé definis, and who say the most disconnected things only for the sake of being able to use all the persons in the tense which for the time being happens to be the subject of conversation, while they carefully postpone the use of the subjunctive until next year' (1947:17-8). The artificial view of language the pupil will get after such treatment, will certainly not help him master the language but only some abstract rules.

[2] To get the meaning of a foreign text, several devices can be used, and they are pointed out in Chapter V by the author. Jespersen is very strong in criticizing the use of translation, and in this he clearly dissents from Sweet.

[3] By 'inventional grammar' Jespersen means nothing more than 'inductive grammar' despite Sweet's misunderstanding. The following is Jespersen's defense of his concept: 'Dr. Sweet tries to throw ridicule on my suggestion as to inventional grammar (The Practical Study of Languages, 1899, pp. 115-116); he seems to forget the distinction between independent grammatical research and teaching in schools; and when he speaks about the boys having to sort "a hundredweight or so of slips", I think his exaggeration needs no further refutation than the above statements which are nothing but an amplification of what I wrote in 1886. Fortunately, on p. 117, Dr. Sweet recommends practically the same course

as is outlined here, only carried out to a less extent' (1947:133, note 1).

4 Jespersen gave an example of how this principle should be applied by treating morphology and syntax together in his own little English grammar (1903). For a discussion of the concept of 'functional grammar' cf. R. Titone (1965:373, note 19).

5 The whole of Chapter X is a very detailed description of practical procedures of teaching pronunciation, most of which can be usefully retained even today. Particularly interesting is the demonstration offered by Jespersen between pp. 146 and 152 on the way a lesson in phonetics for younger pupils can be effec- tively simplified while retaining its scientific exactness.

6

HAROLD E. PALMER

The span between linguistic theory and teaching practice was most effectively bridged by Harold E. Palmer (1877-1949). Sweet and Jespersen, no matter how practically inclined, were and remained chiefly linguists, whereas Palmer was mainly a teacher. Palmer's active and productive career was summarized in a beautiful commemorative article published by Daniel Jones shortly after his death, at 72, in 1949.[1] (Cf. Jones, 1950). The following biographical note is based almost entirely on Jones's article.

Harold E. Palmer was educated first privately by his father and then at a school at Hythe in Kent where he carried off all possible prizes. In his early teens he was sent for some time to Boulogne to learn to speak French, where he spent most of his time in the art gallery painting in oils. He did, however, become a proficient French speaker. On his return to England, he joined the staff of a local newspaper owned by his father, and contributed articles on various subjects. He also became an expert on typography and the processes of printing. This practical-mindedness aided him throughout his life, particularly in the field of language teaching.

In 1902 he was eager to go abroad, and joined a branch of the Berlitz School of Languages at Viviers, Belgium. He soon discovered weak points in that method of language teaching, so he worked out a method of his own, and before long set up his own school of languages, where he taught mainly English and French.

Palmer had an original, inventive mind. In these early days he invented, among other things, a card index system for helping students to learn languages. Instructions and exercises were printed on one side of each card, and solutions were provided on the reverse side. From the first, he made considerable use of phonetics, and for some years used a transcription of his own devising, in which he used accents borrowed from the French system of distinguishing shades of vowel sound; for instance, he used the notation é to denote the English diphthong ei. It was in 1907 that he first heard of the Phonetic Association, which he joined in July of that year. He realized the superiority of the 'new letter' system, and very soon discarded his own transcription in favor of the phonetic alphabet, which he thereafter employed exclusively. [1]

When Viviers was invaded in 1914, Palmer stayed on undiscovered for six weeks, and then managed to escape with his wife and young daughter into Holland. He went to England and started a school for teaching English to refugees at Folkestone. After some months he decided to move to London and obtained an appointment as French master in a London secondary school. In October 1915, he was invited to deliver a course of evening lectures on methods of language teaching at University College, London. These lectures attracted large audiences, mainly school teachers, and were the forerunners of many successful courses. In 1916, he was appointed a regular member of the staff at the department of phonetics at University College, a position which he occupied with distinction until 1921. During this period he wrote several books of note (see the bibliography).

In 1921 he received an invitation from the Japanese Ministry of Education to go to Japan to study and improve the teaching of English in that country. He left for Tokyo early in 1922, and by lectures, demonstrations, and writing books, carried out his duties with conspicuous success. Soon after his arrival he found a need for closer cooperation not only with the officials of the Ministry but also with all Japanese, British, and American teachers of English in the country. To achieve this, on his recommendation there was founded at Tokyo in 1923 the Institute for Research in English Teaching, for which accommodations and a small staff were provided in the Department of Education. Palmer was appointed director of the institute and editor of its bulletin, which appeared ten times a year. Periodic meetings were held to discuss problems in the practical teaching of English. These meetings were fruitful and were attended by teachers from every part of Japan.

While in Japan, Palmer took an interest in the question of romanic spelling for the Japanese language, and in 1930 he wrote a remarkable book which contributed greatly to the clarification of the problems involved.

In 1935 the Imperial University of Tokyo honored Palmer by conferring on him the degree of 'Bungaku Hakushi' (Doctor of Literature) in recognition of the scholarly work displayed in his Grammar of Spoken English and English Intonation.

He left Japan in 1936 and returned to England where, in country surroundings, he wrote a number of other books mostly designed for foreign learners of English. In spite of his poor health and family sorrows (his son, an aircraft pilot, died in battle in 1942), he undertook a lecture tour in South America in 1944.

Palmer published over a hundred books, pamphlets, and articles. Many dealt with the structure of language and the improvement of teaching methods; others were books for class use.[2] It is not possible here to give any full account of these works, but Palmer took particular interest in two subjects—the grading of vocabulary and intonation. D. Jones remembered him, in 1915, giving an illuminating lecture on the limitation of vocabulary, in which he exhibited some well thought-out word lists prepared independently of any work that was being done by others in the same field.[3] The subject of intonation first attracted his attention in 1917. Here he was not a pioneer, since the way had already been paved to some extent by H. Klinghardt and H. O. Coleman. But his book on the subject, English Intonation with Systematic Exercises (Cambridge, 1922), according to Jones, an outstanding authority in the field, considerably extended our knowledge of this interesting branch of phonetics. The book was full of original observations, and in it Palmer demonstrated for the first time his ingenious system of tone-markers.[4] For years afterward, he continued to collect data on intonation, some of which were incorporated in his New Classification of English Tones (Tokyo, 1933).

Palmer had many interests outside his professional work. He was interested in artificial languages, and learned both Esperanto and Ido; he considered the latter far superior. He was an amateur geologist and amassed a good collection of fossils. On one occasion he made a geological model of the Isle of Wight, which he presented to the department of geology at University College, London. He was an advocate of duodecimal numbering and invented the names mem and koo for the numbers designated by 11 and 12 in the English decimal system.

Palmer definitely overcame the lack of direction and systematization that had characterized the direct method at the end of the nineteenth century. Practical methodology finally appeared to be logically tied to and derived from linguistic and psychological theory, while bearing at the same time the marks of successful classroom testing.

The following bibliographic list includes some of Palmer's numerous publications particularly worth studying:

Colloquial English (1916)
The Scientific Study and Teaching of Languages (1917)
A First Course of English Phonetics (1917)
The Principles of Language-Study (1921)
The Oral Method of Teaching Languages (1921)
English Intonation with Systematic Exercises (1922)
A Grammar of Spoken English on a Strictly Phonetic Basis
   (1924)
A Dictionary of English Pronunciation with American Vari-
   ants. With J. Victor Martin and F. G. Blandford. In
   phonetic transcription. (1926)
Everyday Sentences in Spoken English (1927)
The Principles of Romanization with Special Reference to
   Japanese (1931)
A New Classification of English Tones (1933)
The Principles of English Phonetic Notation (1934)
A Grammar of English Words (1938)
The Teaching of Oral English (1940)
The Five Speech-Learning Habits (1948)
H.E.P. and Palmer, Dorothée, English through Actions
   (1959)

Even a quick glance at this partial list of publications brings out Palmer's exceptional contribution to the teaching of English as a foreign language and, indirectly, to the larger field of language teaching methodology.

General methodological orientation

Palmer's general orientation in the methodology of foreign language teaching can be best understood by bringing into relief the three foundational systems of principles on which he built his method—linguistics, psychology, and pedagogy. All three in his opinion were equally important.

Palmer's ambition was to build a true and complete science of language teaching in contrast to the empirical or partially scientific trends of his early days. A science of language study is possible only by integrating into one coherent system the principles derived from three independent sciences, namely linguistics (analysis of phonetical, grammatical, and lexicological facts), pedagogy (value of concretization in teaching), psychology (the laws of memory).[5]

A science of this kind should be useful to methodologists, teachers, and students, for it would supply them with clearly defined universal principles and make for greater economy of effort and efficiency.

The Scientific Study and Teaching of Languages is a comprehensive theoretical treatise on methodology. Its aim is to justify, develop, and apply along general lines the basic principles of a scientific method. In trying to summarize the data offered by the three disciplines mentioned above, we shall at first follow the contents of this book.

(1) Linguistics as a scientific basis of method. The science of language, and not literature, should be the first basis of a language teaching method. 'The learning of foreign languages', writes Palmer, 'must proceed on a philological [linguistic] basis and not on a literary one, because before we can learn the foreign literature we must be acquainted with the language itself, just as when we started learning the literary form of our own tongue we were already acquainted with the language itself' (SSTL:32). Linguistics offers the language teacher not only useful data, but also a means of selecting it.

Palmer means by linguistics the analytic description of language as 'a series of natural phenomena'. The data from linguistics can be generally classified as follows:

Lexicology studies:
    monologs (single separate words)
    polylogs (word-groups)
    miologs (functional units: affixes, inflexions)
    alogisms (position, stress, intonation, sousentendus)

(n.b. Palmer insists that one should avoid speaking of words as autonomous units.)

Morphology studies:
    sounds (phonetics)
    phonemes (phonology)
    letters (orthography)
    etymons (etymology)

Semantic studies:
  semanticons (units of signification)
  semantic groups (groups of synonyms)
  definitions (a polylogical synonym of a shorter unit)
  translations (foreign synonyms of native units)

Ergonics[6] studies:
  ergons (units of grammatical function)
   under the aspect of composition:
    sentences (decomposables)
    insecables (undecomposables)
   under the aspect of special function:
    finites
    infinites
    auxiliaries
    modifiers
    adjuncts, etc.

This classification should help the teacher get an orderly view of the facts of language and enable him to distribute and grade properly the linguistic material to be presented at the various stages of a language course. But the isolated units created by linguistic analysis cannot be transferred as such into practical teaching. Teaching has to put the student in contact with the living language, and therefore with functioning wholes or structures. This is tantamount to saying that lexicon and grammar cannot be separated in the actual study of language. 'The two subjects are bound up with each other and interdependent, and ... they can only be differentiated by doing violence to each. The words themselves and their attendant phenomena cannot be separated except by invoking the arbitrary' (SSTL:32-3). This concept, which had already been voiced by Jespersen, constitutes for Palmer the basic principle of applied linguistics.

(2) The psychological analysis of the language learning process as the second foundation to methodology.[7] Palmer, borrowing concepts and laws from the psychology of his day, attempted to sketch out an elementary analysis of the process of learning a language. Fundamentally, he regarded learning the language skills as a 'process of unconscious assimilation' (PLS:6). Of course, this definition concerns specifically the practical use of the spoken language. He observes: 'We are all endowed by nature with certain capacities which enable each of us, without the exercise of our powers of study, to assimilate and to use the spoken form of

any colloquial language, whether native or foreign' (PLS:11). These practical powers are often disregarded and left latent, but can also be advantageously cultivated. Practical learning is, therefore, based on direct contact with the language, frequency of listening, and repetition, as can be observed in the child's learning of the mother tongue.

On the other hand, learning to write and read, learning the higher or more artificial forms of language, correcting erroneous learnings, acquiring a theoretical knowledge of the language, all these and other more conscious abilities require the use of what Palmer calls our 'studial capacities' (PLS:ch. 3). These are all those forms of activity that demand conscious efforts of attention, analysis and synthesis, 'conversion activities',[8] the use of the eye, and the like.[9]

In conclusion, language study cannot be either a purely practical process, still less a random process (a 'natural approach'), or a purely theoretical work of the intellect. 'Language study is such a complex thing, with so many aspects, and it requires to be looked at from so many points of view, that we must enlist all our capacities when striving to obtain the mastery we desire; we must not neglect our spontaneous powers, nor should we despise our intellectual powers; both are of service to us, both have their place in a well-conceived programme of study, each will to a certain extent balance the other and be complementary to it. An excess on either side may be prejudicial to the student, and one of the more important problems before the speech-psychologist is to determine in what circumstances and on what occasions each should be used' (PLS:22). This is what Palmer called in the final section of his book, The Principles of Language-Study, a 'multiple line of approach' (chapter 15).

(3) Pedagogical considerations are the third basis of methodology (SSTL, part III). The pedagogical method stems from the consideration of the aims to be attained, some important subjective factors, some equally important objective factors, and the importance of the elementary or initial stage.

The definition of the aims of language study will necessarily determine the choice of the way of teaching. 'A complete and ideal language method has a fourfold object, and this is to enable the student, in the shortest possible time and with the least effort, so to assimilate the materials of which the foreign language is composed that he is thereby enabled to understand what he hears and reads, and also to express himself correctly both by the oral and written mediums' (SSTL:47; cf. also p. 71).

Second, 'in order to determine the best programme for a given student we must take into consideration four subjective factors: (a) the student; (b) his previous study of the language; (c) his preliminary equipment; (d) his incentive' (SSTL:48). The importance of the student's capacities and especially of his linguistic aptitude cannot be underestimated (SSTL:48-50). But no less relevant is the end or aim of the individual student. 'The best method is that which adopts the best means to the required end' (PLS:23; cf. also chapter 4).

Third, some objective factors will require special attention in language study, particularly the following: '(a) the language to be studied; (b) the orientation of the study; (c) the extent of the study; (d) the degree of the study; (e) the manner of the study' (SSTL:58). First, the language to be studied by its very nature and structure may pose particular problems. Both contrasts and similarities between the learner's native language and the foreign language can raise difficulties, and similarities may be the more deceitful. 'The absence of morphological resemblance tends to a sounder system of study. A pupil', Palmer believes, 'will be more docile and require fewer disciplinary measures when learning a language of a totally strange nature' (SSTL:59). By 'orientation' Palmer means the variety of the language (written or spoken), and especially in its passive or active use (SSTL:65 ff.).

Finally, the supreme importance of the elementary stage should be well emphasized, for it is this stage which must first 'enable the student to make use, even if only in a rudimentary way, of the language he is learning' and second so 'prepare the student that his subsequent rate of progress shall constantly increase.' 'The function of the first language', Palmer rightly observes, 'is not only to teach the language, but, more important still, to teach the student how to learn' (PLS:32-3, cf. whole of chapter 5).

The conclusion is similar to the one drawn from psychology: a good method must be adaptable to all the subjective and objective conditions characterizing the teaching situation.

General principles

In his two methodological treatises Palmer was careful to outline at the start the 'general principles' that were to guide the foreign language teacher in planning an effective course of instruction. An orderly presentation of these basic tenets is to be found

especially in chapters 6 through 16 of his book, The Principles
of Language Study.

(1) Initial preparation. It is important at the beginning to
awaken and develop the student's natural or spontaneous capacities for language study by means of appropriate forms of exercise. There are definite disadvantages in starting with theory. [10]
On the other hand, effective practice will induce the student to
try persistently to imitate the successful performances of others.
Therefore, the first task of the teacher will be 'to train the student to form new habits and cause him to refrain from adapting
his old ones in cases where we know that such adaptation will be
fruitless' (PLS:43). Second, it is necessary 'to train ourselves
(or our students) consciously to learn unconsciously; we must
set out deliberately to inhibit our capacities for focusing or concentrating our attention on the language-material itself. Attention must be given to what we want to say and not to the way we
say it' (PLS:44). Along this line Palmer proposes special exercises for ear training, articulation, and mimicry (PLS:45-7).
Third, we must reach the ability of 'understanding the gist of
what we hear without any intervention of analysis or synthesis'
(PLS:50). To this end appropriate exercises are suggested by
Palmer (PLS:50 ff.).

(2) Habit forming and habit adapting. The paramount importance of habit in language control is duly stressed by Palmer. As
a consequence, repetition is necessary for automatization; but it
must be carried on in attractive and interesting ways, sometimes
by utilizing certain previously acquired habits. [11] Varied repetition can be achieved by employing 'substitution tables' which
Palmer used frequently. [12] Once the basic patterns have been
memorized, the student becomes able to construct new materials
in the foreign language. [13]

(3) Accuracy. It is defined as 'conformity with a given
standard or model' (PLS:61). The branches of language study in
which there can be accuracy or inaccuracy are: sounds, stress
and intonation, fluency, orthography, sentence-building, inflex-
ions, meanings (PLS:63-4). The principle that is to guide the
teacher in ensuring accuracy should be: 'Do not allow the student
to have opportunities for inaccurate work until he has arrived at
the stage at which accurate work is to be reasonably expected'
(PLS:64). The means of achieving this goal are a good knowledge
of linguistic science and proper gradation of exercises.

(4) Gradation consists in 'passing from the known to the unknown by easy stages, each of which serves as a preparation for

the next' (PLS:67). It is to be applied in the distribution and presentation of both the grammatical and the lexical material. The
basic criterion for grading such material shall be 'usefulness'.
'The vocabulary in a well-graded language-course', Palmer sug-
gests, 'will be arranged in such a manner that the more useful
words will be learnt before the less useful' (PLS:67). The usefulness of a word should be judged on the basis of its meaning and its
role as a sentence-former.[14] Gradation has an all-embracing
value, since it should be applied to all levels of language learning, as is shown by the following enumeration of dependent rules:
'Ears before eyes.' 'Reception before production.' 'Oral repetition before reading.' 'Immediate memory before prolonged
memory.' 'Chorus-work before individual work.' 'Drill-work
before free work.' (PLS:71-74).

(5) Proportion means paying the right amount of attention to:
all the four skills of language usage; all the branches of practical
linguistics (phonetics, orthography, word-building, sentence-
building, and semantics); all the desiderata in the choice of
vocabulary material; all the useful types of exercises (PLS:79-80).

(6) Concreteness means teaching more by example than by
precept. 'Observe the principle of concreteness by using examples, many examples, cumulative examples, real examples, and
examples embodying the personal interest' (PLS:86).

(7) Interest is certainly needed for successful learning, but
the quality of the teaching should not suffer on that account.
Palmer discusses six factors that promote interest (PLS:91 ff.):
elimination of bewilderment, a sense of achievement, competition,
game-like exercises, a good relation between teacher and pupil,
and variety.

(8) A rational order of progression is important; the teacher
must establish the order in which the various aspects and branches
of a language should be dealt with. At this point some vexing
questions arise, which cannot always be solved definitively. Here
are some examples of such questions. Do written or spoken exercises come first? Shall we start with systematic ear-training
and articulation exercises? Shall we admit or reject the use of
phonetic transcription? Should we teach intonation in the early
stages? Are words or sentences to be handled first? Should irregularities be included or excluded during the earlier stages? Is
immediate fluency or gradual fluency the goal? The grammar-
translation tradition would solve these problems differently than
the modern trend. Two contrasting orders of progression result:

THE ANCIENT ORDER
Based on tradition

First, learn how to convert 'dictionary-words' (i.e. etymons) into 'working sentence-units' (i.e. ergons). This will be done by memorizing the rules of derivation.

Secondly, learn the general structure of sentences. This will be done chiefly by reading and translation exercises.

Third, memorize the irregular or idiomatic phenomena of the language.

Last, (if necessary) convert the 'eye-knowledge' of the language into 'ear-knowledge' by means of reading aloud and by 'conversation-lessons'.

THE MODERN ORDER
Based on psychology

First, become proficient in recognizing and in producing foreign sounds and tones, both isolated and in combinations.

Secondly, memorize (without analysis or synthesis) a large number of complete sentences chosen specifically for this purpose by the teacher or by the composer of the course.

Third, learn to build up all types of sentences (both regular and irregular) from 'working sentence-units' (i.e. ergons) chosen specifically for this purpose by the teacher or by the composer of the course.

Last, learn how to convert 'dictionary-words' (i.e. etymons) into 'working sentence-units' (i.e. ergons).

'All our experience', Palmer declares, 'leads us to endorse most emphatically all the statements made in the right-hand column' (PLS:105). Any modern applied linguist can easily agree with Palmer when he says that 'a rational order of progression will not only rapidly secure useful and desirable results, but will also encourage the formation of the right sort of language-habits and ensure as a permanent result the capacity for using the foreign language in the fullest sense of the term' (PLS:107).

Special principles

The general features listed above as characteristic of a modern course of language instruction are indicative of a well conceived method. Linguistics and psychology jointly underlie all
the principles previously mentioned. The 'special principles' to
which we now turn are the ultimate articulation of Palmer's
method and show more clearly the influence of linguistics, psychology, and especially pedagogy. They are expounded in detail
in The Scientific Study and Teaching of Languages.

(1) Segregation (SSTL:72 ff.).[15] 'In order to exclude confusion and misunderstanding, during the initial period of conscious
study the phonetic, orthographic, etymological, semantic, and
ergonic aspects of language must be segregated from each other
and taught independently. In the process of subconscious study,
and in the later periods of conscious study, such segregation is
neither possible nor desirable' (SSTL:72). After the first global
contact with the language at which time sentences are memorized
as wholes, it becomes necessary to analyze what has been
learned and penetrate its structure. Difficulties usually arise
from confused perceptions or confused thoughts during the global
learning. Segregation is offered as the proper remedy.

(2) Passive assimilation before active work. This principle
is grounded in the psychology of first language learning. 'The
young child only comes to speak his native language after an "incubation period", during which he has passively received and
stored up in his mind a considerable quantity of linguistic material. The same process may profitably be employed by the more
adult person in the study of foreign languages' (SSTL:75). Hence,
'we would suggest that one of the essential principles of all methods designed on the "natural" basis should be never to encourage
nor expect the active production of any linguistic material until
the pupil has had many opportunities of cognizing it passively. If
this principle is valid, then most of the teaching of the present
day violates a natural law!' (SSTL:77). Accordingly, the order
of study will be: first listening, then speaking; first reading,
then writing.

(3) Ways of 'semanticizing'. Palmer coined the term 'semanticizing' to mean 'the conveying of meanings'. 'There are four
different manners or modes of conveying to the pupil the meaning
of a given unit: (a) by material association, i.e. associating the
unit with that which is designated by it; (b) by translation, i.e.
associating the unit with the equivalent native unit; (c) by definition,

i.e. associating the unit with its definition of paraphrase (i.e. its polylogical equivalent); (d) by context, i.e. giving examples of its use' (SSTL:77). There are different procedures of applying the four ways of semanticizing (SSTL:78 ff.).

One important point made by Palmer in this context is his defense of the value of translation as a way of semanticizing. The following are the reasons he invokes.

(a) 'Translation is a more direct mode of conveying the meaning of a unit than Definition, and, a fortiori, more direct than context' (SSTL:88). However, as he goes on to explain: 'When the foreign word to be demonstrated is known to be a doubtful equivalent or when the value of the equivalence is unknown, it is more prudent to confirm the translation by definition or by context; when the word to be demonstrated is known to have no equivalent whatever in the native tongue, then we must have recourse to definition or to context' (SSTL:91). Of course, Palmer thinks that definition in the native tongue would be the best type of translation taken in a wider sense, inasmuch as it can guarantee safety from all possible ambiguity.

(b) 'The exclusion of translation as a regular means of conveying the meaning of units is an uneconomical and unnatural principle' (SSTL:93). In fact, translating is unavoidable whenever one is confronted with unknown units in a foreign language.[16] The main caution to be observed by the student should be to avoid building equivalences between isolated items in the native and in the foreign tongue. Good translation generally involves equivalences of larger units.

In spite of Palmer's strong plea for the re-introduction of translation as a semanticizing procedure, his balanced view of the problem leads him to a relativistic attitude. 'No hard and fast rule', he clearly states, 'can be adopted as to the mode of giving the meanings of units: each in its turn may be superior to the others' (SSTL:100).

(4) Learning by heart (catenizing). 'Learning by heart is the basis of all linguistic study, for every sentence ever uttered or written by anybody has either been learnt by heart in its entirety or else has been composed (consciously or subconsciously) from smaller units, each of which must at one time have been learnt by heart. We may term 'primary matter' all units learnt by heart integrally, and 'secondary matter' all units built up or derived by the pupil from primary matter' (SSTL:103).

The heavy reliance on memorization is justified on two counts:

(a) 'The progress of the student can only be measured by his capacity for understanding and producing fluent sentences ... Modern psychologists incline toward the "integral theory", and can produce data showing that a given "chain" is more quickly memorized in its entirety than when we memorize its "links" one by one' (SSTL:103).

(b) There are definite advantages in assimilating 'integral units' rather than deriving secondary matter by inference (by means of grammatical theory). First, all possibility of error is excluded, since the right construction is directly established. Second, the student is relieved from the burden of abstract calculation.[17] Third, the immediate utility of matter so learned is self-evident.

The emphasis placed by Palmer on memorization, while fully justified,[18] should not lead the modern reader to think that he denied the creative side of speech and the transformational aspects of language, emphasized by certain schools of linguistics today. He believed that the starting point in the use of language is the automatized mastery of some basic materials, lexical and grammatical patterns, which will become the basis for further combinations and transformations which Palmer called 'conversions'.

Evaluation of Palmer's contribution

After this brief summary of Palmer's ideas there can be no doubt about the unique importance of his contribution to language teaching methodology. While keeping a fine sense of balance and moderation in proposing progressive procedures, Palmer went beyond the achievements of Sweet and Jespersen. His closeness to the sophisticated views of contemporary applied linguistics is striking.

The following quotation seems to summarize Palmer's thinking:

We use the eye before we use the ear; we take up writing before we take up speaking; we teach reading before we teach pronouncing; we study the rules before we study the examples; we concentrate on quantity before we concentrate on quality. In all this, our error is that we go against the facts of language. A language is first of all 'speech'—a system of sounds transmitted directly from mouth to ear and produced by automatic reactions of the speech organs. The functioning of those automatic reactions depends on the linguistic habits of the speaker, and it is the acquisition of these habits that must come first. Therefore, in order to be efficient in teaching oral expression, pronunciation and grammar, we must strive to form: (1) Psychological habits of associating sounds directly with meaning and meaning directly with sounds before learning to read. (2) Physiological habits of good pronunciation—articulation and diction—before learning to write. (3) Grammatical habits of morphology and syntax before learning the rules of grammar. Then, efficiency in oral expression, pronunciation and grammar will lead to efficiency in reading and writing and will make for a much deeper acquaintance with culture than only reading and writing could have done.

The author, however, of these lines is not Palmer, but an applied linguist writing a generation later (Delattre 1947:243). But Palmer, even thirty years before, could have endorsed these views and written his signature below such a statement. He had basically the same ideas as most methodologists today; he used the same conceptual vocabulary (but for some neologisms of his own making) that we use today.

The values in Palmer's methodological conception can be easily ascertained. In general, we can consider as fairly successful his attempt to build a scientific methodology of language teaching by basing it on supposedly scientific data drawn from a triad of pertinent sciences (linguistics, psychology, and pedagogy)—what nowadays would be called an 'interdisciplinary approach'. Palmer's responsiveness to modern scientific trends is manifested not only by his demands for a truly scientific description of language, but also by his exploitation of what were considered to be the tested principles of the then accepted psychology of learning and, more particularly, some essential notions concerning the psychology of speech.

In particular, we can appreciate a balanced criticism of both the formal grammatical method and the strict interpretation of the direct method. He saw that language is a system of structures to be learned as wholes. To this end, he stressed the principle of overlearning first the basic patterns (memorization of primary matter) before making creative use of language. Finally, all the general and special principles of foreign language teaching as developed by him especially in his two methodological treatises are useful to this day.

Naturally, Palmer's formulations contain some objectionable aspects. First, certain oddities in his linguistic terminology may have been due to his tendency to work as an independent linguist even though he was familiar with the works of Sweet, Jespersen, De Saussure, and others. Second, some obscurities remain in the notions related to unconscious or subconscious assimilation of language. Palmer's concept could be applied to the end-result of language acquisition, that is, the automatization of verbal responses, but not to the process of acquisition in its entirety itself.

In sum, Harold E. Palmer can rightly be considered one of the greatest methodologists of the first half of our century. Most of his insights have become —sometimes without acknowledgement— permanent acquisitions of contemporary applied linguistics.

NOTES

[1] As Jones testifies, Palmer eventually tried out the IPA in both narrow and broad forms, but it seems that he never came to any conclusion as to the relative merits of the narrow and broad types of transcription.

[2] A complete list was published by H. Bongers (1947:350-3).

[3] 'This was his customary way of working; he seldom utilized anyone else's results to help him to arrive at his conclusions' (D. Jones). Palmer, however, shows the influence of great linguists such as Sweet, Jespersen, and Breal. Moreover, one of his books was probably inspired by a conversation with a friend. 'Shortly after the end of the First World War Palmer had a memorable meeting with an old friend, Charles Lemaire, a specialist in the teaching of French as a foreign language. Palmer, himself an enthusiast, was deeply impressed by Lemaire's fervour and by the similarity of their views. The Principles of Language-Study was written as a direct result of their conversation. In fact he began to write it the same day. The book is, not surprisingly, dedicated to Lemaire' (R. Mackin, editor's preface to the 1964 edition of the book, p. v).

[4] It should be mentioned that the manuscript of this book was completed before the appearance of Klinghardt's Übungen im Englischen Tonfall, in 1920.

[5] The scientific concept of language teaching methodology is defended and developed in Part I of The Scientific Study and Teaching of Languages (1917), hereafter abbreviated SSTL.

[6] 'To cover all the phenomena and operations connected with analysis and synthesis, from the sentence down to the insecable,

and vice versa, we suggest and shall henceforth use the comprehensive term Ergonics' (SSTL:46). Ergonics can be equated
roughly with syntax.

[7] For this part cf. The Principles of Language-Study, 1964
edition, hereafter PLS.

[8] These would be such activities as converting the spoken
into the written language or the reverse, converting something
from one language into another, converting an affirmative sentence into a negative one, passive into active, singular into plural,
etc. (PLS:13).

[9] Chapter 2 of PLS is devoted to a discussion of studial capacities.

[10] Theory will usually lead the student to 'reconstruct' the
foreign language on the basis of rigid rules and will delay his
acquisition of the new language habits. Cf. PLS:40-4.

[11] 'It is for the skillful language-teacher to ascertain which of
the student's known habits can be most nearly adapted to what is
required' (PLS:59). 'A judiciously selected native form will produce better results than a badly constructed foreign form' (PLS:
60, note 1).

[12] Cf. H. E. Palmer, 1916, Colloquial English. Part I, 100
Substitution Tables. In the preliminary remarks to these Tables
the writer explains 'Substitution' as a system whereby a normal and
idiomatic 'sentence can be multiplied almost indefinitely by substituting any of its words or word-groups by others of the same
grammatical family and within certain semantic limits' (p. iii).

[13] From 'memorized matter' to 'constructed matter': cf.
chapter 16.

[14] Hence the idea of statistical frequency counts. The material
so selected and graded would constitute what Palmer called the
'Microcosm' (or quintessence of the language), which would consist of vocabulary selected according to: frequency, ergonic combination, concreteness, proportion, and general expediency. (Cf.
SSTL:122 ff.)

[15] See diagram illustrating the principle of segregation, p. 75.

[16] He proves his statement by an elementary psychological
analysis (SSTL:97).

[17] On pp. 112-13, he demonstrates with an interesting example
that a specific German sentence formed by an English student by
synthetic construction would necessitate twenty-five separate
efforts of the mind.

[18] Palmer quotes a few passages from a little known book,
How To Learn a Language (by Thomas F. Cummings, D.D., New

York, 1916), to show the importance of automatization in lan-guage learning. One significant passage is the following: 'Unless speaking, like piano-playing, is automatically correct, the result is not enjoyable. The only way to ensure this automatic accuracy in pronunciation, vocabulary, and construction is to learn all sorts of sentences, by frequent repetition, until an inaccurate sentence becomes an impossibility. When one has thus memo-rized his sentences they become matrices for thoughts. They are well-formed moulds into which all statements of that charac-ter readily fall. No pains spent on absolutely fixing these in the memory can be too great' (SSTL:120). Obviously, 'pattern prac-tice' is rather old.

7

FOREIGN LANGUAGE TEACHING BEFORE WORLD WAR II

The ideas of Sweet, Jespersen, Palmer, and others did not
have a very wide influence. Most of the teachers ignored the
proposals of the reformers or never heard of them. Others were
bewildered by the clash between new and old. What was the over-
all situation at the end of the nineteenth century and the beginning
of the twentieth? As far as American schools are concerned, a
fairly comprehensive picture of conditions at the turn of the century is presented by the Report of the Committee of Twelve
(1900).

Report of the Committee of Twelve

The appointment of the committee grew out of a request of the
National Educational Association (1896). The chairman was Professor Calvin Thomas, president of the Modern Language Association of America. The aims of the investigation were to consider the position of the modern languages in secondary education,
and to make recommendations for methods of instruction, training of teachers, and other questions connected with the teaching
of the modern languages in the secondary schools and colleges.
A circular was sent out to some 2,500 teachers. Several hundred
replies were received. These replies, as C. Thomas wrote,
taken as a whole, 'give us a picture of somewhat chaotic and be-
wildering conditions' (Report, 1900:1). Further work by subcom-
mittees on specific questions followed (1898). The results were
a critical review of contemporary methods and some pertinent
recommendations and proposals.
The methods used in those days in teaching foreign languages
could be reduced to five: the grammar method, the natural

method, the psychological method, the phonetic method, and the reading method. Each of these showed both advantages and disadvantages.

The conclusion concerning method is significant, especially with regard to the attitude of the twelve members of the committee. It is worth quoting in full:

> If this report were intended to meet ideal conditions, that is, if it were addressed to teachers whose training would permit them to choose freely from the methods that have been described and to combine them with wise discretion, the committee might be disposed ... to make some such recommendations as to the following: For very young children, say, up to the age of ten, the 'natural' or imitative method of the nurse or governess, with some help perhaps from the 'psychological' method. For a course of six years, beginning, say, at the age of twelve, a combination during the first three years of the 'psychological' and 'phonetic' methods, accompanied by some study of grammar; after that a translation of good literature, supplemented by oral practice in the language and written composition. For a four years' course, beginning in the high school, we should recommend a similar procedure, the division between the 'psychological-phonetic' and the 'reading' method coming, however, somewhat earlier, say, after the first year. In combining the 'psychological' and 'phonetic' methods the general plan of the former would be followed, while the latter would be imitated in its treatment of pronunciation and, so far at least as French is concerned, in its use of phonetically transcribed texts. For any shorter course we should advise the 'reading' method, accompanied, however, by scientific training in pronunciation, drill in the rudiments of grammar, and a moderate amount of oral practice' (34-35).

The phrasing of the statements and the footnotes appended to the text of the Report reveal a thoroughly up-to-date awareness of the day's methodological trends. The Twelve stated a balanced position dictated by educational wisdom and practical demands. The method was to be differentiated and adapted according to the learner's age and goals of instruction. The slightly conservative touch of the recommendations and some limitations in outlook and purpose were obviously determined by the existing social conditions and the insufficiently developed scientific method.

Confusion on one hand and compromise on the other were also characteristics of language teaching in Europe—a condition that was to last until World War II began and the need for effective language instruction became imperative. What Vernon Mallinson states with respect to Great Britain can be safely applied also to the whole of Continental Europe. 'Generally speaking, the prac-tice on the Continent and in Scotland was to ensure that the neces-sary discipline of mind involved in the mastery of any language, living or dead, should not be lost to view. In England, chaos followed quickly in the wake of the enthusiasm stimulated by Ripman and his eager band of followers. No attempt was made to integrate the new teaching with the culture pattern of the peo-ple. It was just stuck on, like a hastily crazily pasted poster' (1957:16-17).

Skepticism among the best-intentioned teachers took the form of a compromise, such as the one expressed by one author. 'The purely Direct Method can safely be adopted provided the right type of teacher and class is forthcoming. The method by its very nature presupposes a teacher of intense vitality, of robust health, and one endowed with real fluency in the modern language he teaches. He must be resourceful in the way of gesture and tricks of facial expression, able to sketch rapidly on the black-board, and, in the long teaching day, he must be proof against linguistic fatigue. And he must have bright pupils. My own ex-perience has taught me that in a school of four hundred pupils, only one form in each year—in a school of a thousand, two forms each year—can receive such instruction, and this, provided the teacher is forthcoming.' This author goes on to advocate what he calls a rational method for the average pupil, a compromise method which has as its constant aim to 'teach as Frenchily or Germanly as possible' (Collins 1934:419).

This was a very unfortunate step. As Mallinson notes, 'once the defences were down the rot set in. It was all very well advo-cating a 'compromise' method to retain all that was the best in the Direct Method, to teach as Frenchily or as Germanly as pos-sible, but it left the unexperienced or ill-equipped teacher floun-dering, returning for self-protection to the old translational method, or at the best using to the best of his ability (which usu-ally meant slavishly) the several new courses that now came on to the market in vindication of the trumpeted compromise. Only gradually, in the period between the two wars, by careful experimentation, by taking note of the new developments in the field of psychology and by insisting that clear and unequivocal statements be made as to the aims and purpose of teaching a modern foreign language in our schools was it possible to clear up in some measure the confusion' (1957:19).

François Closset and Adolf Bohlen

Despite the fact that most teachers either remained in or backed into old routine positions, it is to be acknowledged that there were people, both in Europe and in America, who remained faithful to the advancing trend of scientific methodology. Besides H. E. Palmer and O. Jespersen, who worked the whole first half of the present century, educators like F. Closset and A. Bohlen perseveringly pursued the goals of teaching living languages in a living fashion.

The late Belgian, François Closset (1900-64), had a long and successful career as a language scholar. His influence was especially felt in the French-speaking countries. After having taught in several secondary schools in Belgium, he was called in 1934 to the University of Liège to teach Dutch language and literature as well as methodology (didactique des langues vivantes). Not satisfied with mere university teaching, he wrote numerous practical articles and was among the chief promoters of the Belgian Association of Modern Language Teachers and of its official review, the Revue des Langues Vivantes (Tijdschrift voor Levende Talen). When, on the initiative of Georges Roger, the President of the Association des Professeurs de Langues Vivantes (APLV), the Fédération Internationale des Professeurs de Langues Vivantes (FIPLV) was founded in August 1939, Closset organized a successful international Conference at Liège. The outbreak of World War II did not interrupt Closset's activity. During the German occupation he prepared his important work, Didactique des Langues Vivantes, the result of his lectures since 1929. The first part of the book deals with the basic principles of foreign language teaching (mainly, of psychological derivation); the second part treats extensively of practical procedures, chiefly issuing from a wide range of systematic experiences; the third considers teaching aids (Realia and the like).[1] After the war he devoted all his energies to reviving the International Federation of Foreign Language Teachers by breaking down national barriers. The first international conference of modern language teachers after the war, organized by Closset, was held in

Brussels, July 31-August 3, 1948, and it took place in an atmos-
phere of warm friendship. The Federation had revived with
Closset as its president. He held this post until 1952. During
his chairmanship other national associations were affiliated to
the International Federation, thus tightening the bonds of international cooperation. On the occasion of the international conference organized by UNESCO on 'the teaching of modern languages and international understanding' at Muwara Eliya (Ceylon)
in August 1953, he prepared a long report packed with interesting
information and recommendations. His lasting contribution was
the unification of the efforts of all language teachers, especially
in Europe, toward building a more mature consciousness of contemporary methodological renewal. Although Closset did not
contribute to theoretical methodology, he had enough open-
mindedness and versatility to be able to assimilate readily all the
best suggestions coming both from science and from experience.
A 'pragmatic-eclectic orientation' might be a definition of his
methodology.

Another active language specialist is the German Adolf Bohlen.
Like Closset, he has been a practical organizer in the language
teaching profession for several decades, but, perhaps more than
Closset, he has also kept up with modern developments in the
field of linguistics. Like Closset, he is convinced that languages
must be taught not only for a directly practical purpose, but also
for humanistic purposes. Bohlen has been director of the Landes-
Institut für Neue Sprachen in Münster, Westphalia, and president
of the Deutsches Neuphilologenverband. His name has been held
in esteem not only in Germany, but also in other countries since
he was made president of the International Federation of Modern
Language Teachers. His ideas have been spread by numerous
articles and especially one important book. The first draft,
Neusprachlicher Unterricht (Leipzig, 1930), represented mainly
the ideas cultivated by the German tradition. Its more recent
editions, under the title Methodik des neusprachlichen Unterrichts,
have incorporated developments in foreign language teaching that
have taken place in many countries in Europe and in America
since World War II. Bohlen's perspective is first humanistic and
historical. He believes in the continuity of methodological development through history. He believes in the validity of the contributions of the modern science of linguistics (especially phonetics
and phonology) and in the value of systematic teaching experience.
His manual is a systematic articulate treatment of the essential
phases of foreign language teaching (particularly with respect to

the teaching of English and French) starting from clearly defined goals and theoretical principles and proceeding to practical suggestions. The keynote of the whole approach is sounded in one of the last chapters, where the author declares the importance of reaching an understanding of the 'spirit' of a language through the acquisition of its 'form' 'Von der Sprachform zum Sprachgeist'.

Men like Closset and Bohlen are representative of an age of transition. The decades that preceded World War II were characterized by ingenious attempts mingled with confusion on the practical plane. The conversion of language teaching methodology into a science had started with Sweet, Jespersen, and Palmer, but it took about five decades before that process of conversion could reach satisfactory results. Until the 1940's, teaching practice was still largely arbitrary: some good wheat was mixed with a lot of chaff. However, some salient facts are worth recalling.

General Language and the Cleveland Plan

One experiment, now almost entirely forgotten, was the introduction of 'General Language' into the Detroit schools.[2] It was supposed to be a sort of elementary linguistics at the high school level. In 1918, an experiment substituted 'general language' for English in the seventh grade. The first textbook was Leonard and Cox, General Language (1925). Several other textbooks followed.

In the beginning it was meant to be an exploratory course to determine pupils' aptitude for foreign language study. But it was soon found to be time-wasting and ineffective for this purpose. The shift in purpose is announced in the following statement: 'The real worth of the course will be revealed in its synthesis of the language arts, in its presentation of language as the prime means of human communication, as the most vital and all-pervasive of the instruments of civilization' (Blancké 1939: 80).

General Language was a survey course in the basic principles of language structure and development considered historically and comparatively. It was a course in English and its foreign elements and at the same time a gateway to foreign-language study. It was also a tie between English and the social studies. 'The purpose', as declared by Lindquist, ' is to make pupils language conscious and to build up broad interests by increasing their knowledge and understanding as well as by developing attitudes and appreciations' (1940:563).

The content was not to be specific but was to include general notions and principles applicable to language study. 'This course is not organized for the purpose of teaching specific subject matter. The pupils should be measured by their growth in ability to use language more effectively, to think and to express thought more clearly, to read and to interpret more accurately what they read ... Therefore, a variety of activities is suggested to give ample scope for individual progress in a practically unlimited field' (Lindquist 1940:564).

The course was expected to foster maturity in language and maturity through language. It ought to be said, however, that with such a program there might be a gap between the level of the course contents and their presentation on the one hand and the mental development of the high school student on the other.

Another development of the early twentieth century was called the 'Cleveland Plan', begun in that city in 1919.[3] It was linked to the name of a pioneer of the oral method, Dr. Emile B. de Sauzé. Its principles are explained in de Sauzé's book and applied in his elementary text, Cours pratique de français pour commençants. It is a multiple integrated approach, in which all the four basic language skills are taught simultaneously on the basis of the student's real life experiences. The method was not based on mere memorization, but it implied a firm foundation of grammar taught in a concrete and functional manner.

The main principles of the Cleveland Plan are the following:

(1) The principle of logical challenge. Grammar is not presented, as it were, 'on a platter', but rather inductively, that is, a few carefully chosen illustrations of a given grammatical difficulty are presented, from which the student, with the guidance of his instructor, can induce the law governing the point in question. Vocabulary is learned from context or by paraphrasing.

(2) The principle of single emphasis. The student is confronted with only one difficulty at a time, and abundantly drilled in each rule.

(3) The principle of stimulation. Gradual practical mastery of the foreign language gives the student a stimulating sense of achievement, peculiar to the oral approach, which the ability to read alone can never give him.

The results of the experiment were quite good. Oral performance was excellent, and reading ability did not suffer.[4] The reason was that intensive reading was emphasized rather than extensive reading.

A Demonstration School met each summer under de Sauzé's direction on the Mather Campus of Western Reserve University. Classes were given on all levels of French, German, and Spanish, from kindergarten to university level. For French students, there were also three hours a day of 'French life'. Excellent articulation between these courses and the undergraduate and graduate classes at the university was a notable feature. High school students trained in French could attend college classes in which only the French language was used. These were literature courses and courses in practical French, with vocabulary building, syntax, advanced stylistics, and applied phonetics.

A large measure of credit for success was due to the excellent foreign language teachers and to the expert guidance of Dr. de Sauzé. The plan was still alive in 1945.

De Sauzé's method had a strong psychological bias because it was aimed at teaching young students, while there was no evident attention to the contribution of linguistic analysis.[5] De Sauzé was clearly influenced by the French 'direct-methodists', especially with regard to the 'artistic' concept of language teaching, based mainly on psychological ingenuities or tricks. The teacher's role becomes that of a magician.

The Modern Foreign Language Study

Apart from these ingenious attempts, what was the situation of foreign language teaching in the United States during the 1920's? An answer to this question was given at the end of the period by the so-called 'Modern Foreign Language Study' (Cf. Coleman 1929).

The Modern Foreign Language Study was organized in the spring of 1924 for the purpose of making a general inquiry into the teaching and learning of modern languages in the United States. It was sponsored and financed by the Carnegie Corporation. It was carried on by a committee on direction and control, an executive committee, special investigators (A. Coleman, Ch. A. Purin, C. A. Wheeler), and an advisor in educational psychology (V. A. C. Henmon). The survey was directed to foreign language teaching in the secondary school and the first and second years of college. Large quantities of data were gathered, especially on the measurement of linguistic achievement. The study was to be the introduction to a prolonged program of research. During the winter and spring of 1925 the work consisted in the gathering of enrollment data, in the construction and standardization of objective tests in French, German, and Spanish. These tests were administered during 1925-26 and 1926-27. In addition, special studies were launched and statements of opinion were secured from teachers. This investigation also utilized previous studies such as the Report of the Classical Investigation (Part I) and the experimental study on bilingualism made by Michael West.

The questions the Modern Foreign Language Study was expected to answer were:

(1) Who should and who should not study modern languages?
(2) When should the subject be begun?
(3) What is the minimum time for the profitable study of a modern language?
(4) What should be the specific objectives, in language abilities and in other ways, of the course for the three chief groups involved under present conditions:
(a) Those who study one year at most?
(b) Those who study two years at most?
(c) Those who study three years or more?
(5) What should be the content of the course by years (grammar, vocabulary, reading matter, cultural content) for each of the three groups of students?
(6) What classroom procedures must be followed in order that the objectives may be attained in the most cases?
(7) What standards of achievement may be reasonably expected at the various stages?

Not all these questions could receive a satisfactory answer. What may interest today's methodologists is the summary of the conclusions on method (Coleman 1929:276-7). They can be condensed as follows:

(1) A maximum amount of practice should be allotted to accomplishing the objectives of a particular course.

(2) No single method appears to be superior to all others. However, some form of 'direct' approach has apparently been beneficial.

(3) One cause of poor results in developing oral ability is the inability of teachers to speak the languages they teach.

(4) Success depends not on method alone, but on a variety of factors, such as the organization of the work, the kind of supervision in the departments, the quality of the teaching, and administrative cooperation.

(5) New procedures are needed to develop reading power (under typical American school conditions).

In conclusion, the study came out with a fundamental bias in favor of the 'reading method' as the only one applicable in American schools at that time.[6] This bias was strengthened by the acceptance of M. West's opinion about the importance of reading in learning a foreign language. The survey was too large in scope to yield controlled results. It showed inadequate theoretical background, unlike the Report of Twelve. The main positive point in the study was its recommendations concerning teacher training and linguistic revision of materials (by word counts, studies on syntax, etc.). In short, the Modern Foreign Language Study did not go one step beyond the older Report of Twelve. After thirty years, the situation seemed not only un-changed, but deplorably stagnant.

NOTES

[1] 'L'auteur y examine les problèmes que pose l'enseignement des langues, notamment dans son pays où le bilinguisme com-plique les choses; il indique des solutions dictées par sa riche expérience, son profond bon sens, sa réflexion, sans idées pré-conçues, sans dogmatisme. Rien de rigide dans ses conseils, un sens aigu par contre de la psychologie des jeunes, de ce qui peut les inciter à l'étude des langues, ce qu'Américains et Anglais appellent motivation. Un désir aussi de faire que cet enseigne-ment ne soit pas, seulement ou avant tout, pratique, utilitaire; que de fois l'avons nous vu revenir sur sa valeur formative et culturelle ...' (1965:763-4).

[2] Cf. Lindquist (1940) and Blancké (1939).

[3] Cf. de Sauzé (1929) and McClain (1945).

[4] On the Knight Test, given in 1929, on the French Test of the American Council on Education given in combination with parts of the Cheydleur French Test (1930-33), and on the Cooperative Test of Columbia University given over a period of several years, Cleveland language students scored well above the national norms in reading and comprehension.

[5] In de Sauzé's book (pp. 8-21) one can find a detailed illustra-tion of nineteen particular characteristics of the plan. It can be easily seen that these principles (such as interest, incubation, correct association, activity) were mainly of psychological deriva-tion.

[6] Cf. Coleman (1929:170). However, three members of the Committee on Direction and Control, namely Messrs. Hohlfeld, Roux and de Sauzé, expressed grave doubts as to the validity of

the main conclusion. Their opinion was formulated by Professor Hohlfeld as a criticism of the proposal to increase the reading requirements. This, they said, 'is likely to do more harm than good, and may even prove a step backward in the direction of reading by translation'. (Reported as footnote 1 on page 170 of the final report.)

8

FOREIGN LANGUAGE TEACHING TODAY

It is an historical paradox that a World War was necessary to bring home to many people the widespread need for oral communication and international understanding. The exceptionally rapid development of foreign language teaching methods since 1945 is partly due to this realization. Never was interest in learning foreign languages so intense and widespread as it is today. International communication has been one of the main propulsive factors, but other contributing factors have hastened such development. 'What is new in recent approaches to language-teaching', writes R. Libbish, 'is not the recognition of past errors. It has long been realized that translation develops into a habit, difficult to uproot; and that the speech of most of our pupils has degenerated into a more or less rapid and incorrect process of translation. It was almost true to say that foreign texts were understood less through their own idiom, than through interpretation via the mother tongue. What is new is that, for the first time, scientific investigation has been energetically applied to eradicating these errors, and to substituting in their place a psychological approach linked with linguistic research, and aided by new electronic devices' (1964:viii).

There are so many experiments and trends in language teaching today that it would be difficult for any historian to evaluate each one. Only an overall survey, which will necessarily omit many interesting details, seems feasible here, and that is the aim of the present chapter.

The reform movement, previously limited to a few selected circles in a few countries, has spread all over the eastern and western worlds. One sign of this universality is the rapid emerging of international organizations and the frequency of international

conferences dealing with the problems of modern language teaching. Let us look at the situations in a few selected countries.

The United States

Despite a long interest in language teaching on the part of
American linguists like William Dwight Whitney and Leonard
Bloomfield and of gifted teachers such as those mentioned in the
previous chapters, before 1941 little was done to improve teaching techniques by applying scientific categories and results.
World War II brought to an abrupt end the linguistic isolationism
of the United States. The need was for practical mastery of
many, even exotic, languages, and for intensive, rapid training
of large numbers of individuals, especially in the armed forces.
In early 1941 the American Council of Learned Societies (ACLS)
established an Intensive Language Program aiming first at a
sound linguistic analysis of each language to be taught and then at
the preparation of learning materials based on this analysis. The
armed forces availed themselves of the already existing Intensive
Language Program, and in 1943 the first area and language
courses of the Army Specialized Training Program (ASTP) were
established. The same year, the Army's Civil Affairs Training
Schools (CATS) were established, which gave language and other
training to officers headed for occupation duties in Italy, Germany,
and Japan. It was during this initial period that significant guides
were produced by outstanding American linguists, like Bloomfield's Outline Guide for the Practical Study of Foreign Languages
(1942) and Bloch and Trager's Outline of Linguistic Analysis
(1942).

After the war, most of the features of such linguistic programs
were continued in both army and civilian schools. The Committee
on the Language Program (CLP), an organ of the ACLS, became a
nationwide organization, actively seeking to further the cause of
linguistics. Research in linguistics, summer Linguistic Institutes,
application of linguistics to various fields of activity (machine
translation, computer programs, and especially language teaching), preparation of new textbooks and recorded materials for the
teaching of the spoken language, periodicals, conferences, etc.,
all sprang up.

Most characteristic of the new American methodology is the
influence of modern linguistics on the new ways of language
teaching. There emerged from the linguists' work a set of principles such as the following: 'language is speech, not writing';

'a language is a set of habits'; 'teach the language, not about the language'; 'a language is what its native speakers say, not what someone thinks they ought to say'; 'languages are different'.[2]

Today, the American scene is buzzing with activity. Linguists continue to exert their influence and new names have appeared. There is general agreement that the beginnings of foreign language instruction should be exclusively audio-lingual. The concept of 'area studies' has broadened the notion of culture from a purely artistic and literary concept to one embracing sociology and anthropology. Programmed language instruction is being experimented with on all levels. Since 1952, the Modern Language Association of America, with grants from the Rockefeller Foundation, has been carrying on a Foreign Language Program dealing with the quantitative and qualitative analysis of the teaching of modern languages in the USA, offering guidance in the proper use of the language laboratory, narrowing the breach between linguists and language teachers, establishing bases for cultural analyses, examining the possibilities for programmed language instruction. The Center for Applied Linguistics, established in 1959 in Washington, supported by a grant from the Ford Foundation, has become a clearing house for international exchange of information on the teaching of English as a second language, the study of non-European languages, and the application of descriptive linguistics to classroom teaching of foreign languages. It has also become the chief promoter of international and national meetings to deal with a variety of problems in the field of applied linguistics. Finally, it directs documentary publications and a series of contrastive structural analyses.

Last but not least, the National Defense Education Act (NDEA), passed by the United States Congress in 1948, has given new impetus to the new trend by subsidizing laboratories, research projects, and teacher training. A most important activity of the NDEA has been the establishment of linguistic institutes that offer teachers intensive training in the four language skills, applied linguistics, the culture of foreign countries, and modern methods of teaching, including the use of the language laboratory. The quality of instruction is improved not so much by modern equipment and textbooks as by more efficient training of the language teachers.

In conclusion, E. M. Stack is certainly voicing the common conviction of American language teachers when he states: 'Today's foreign language teaching is achieving success unknown under the traditional methods. This has been accomplished by

the application of structural linguistics to teaching, particularly
in the realms of proper sequence, oral drills, inductive grammar, and the use of pattern drills to give intensive practice. A
major step has been the recognition that language speaking is a
matter of habituation rather than of rational manipulation of
'rules'; and that speaking and understanding must <u>precede</u> the
graphic skills if the foreign language is to be learned thoroughly'
(1964:80-1).

Great Britain

'Language teaching in Britain is in the throes of a revolution'
(Strevens 1965:171). Although famous men such as Sweet, Ripman, Palmer and a host of 'direct-methodologists' were working
before World War II, it has been only recently that the British
schools have undergone deep and sweeping changes. Much has
happened since a special committee, appointed by the Prime
Minister, wrote in its 1918 report: 'Languages are learned for
necessity, profit or intellectual satisfaction. Our necessity was
not apparent, our profit was sufficient, and the most of us found
in other ways such modest intellectual satisfaction as we craved.'
Times have changed since the days of Dr. Arnold, who daringly
decreed that French might be taught at Rugby's Public School in
addition to Latin and Greek, but remarked, prudently, that no
English boy could ever be expected to 'pronounce' French.
Shortly after the 1914 war, a Board of Education report spoke of
schools in which the French expression <u>dites-moi</u> was still pro-
nounced to rhyme with <u>bright boy</u>. However, while foreign language teaching was lagging considerably within England, some
outstanding teachers had found new paths to the teaching of
English as a foreign language. Sooner or later the winds of
change began to blow on foreign language classes, producing a
sudden realignment of purposes and techniques. This has happened mainly during the last fifteen years.
There are reasons for the present renewal in Britain, as a
noted methodologist, Peter Strevens, recently explained. 'Those
days are over, their passing hastened by the great social and
economic changes of the past twenty-five years; by a familiarity
with overseas travel and by the contacts with foreigners which
the Second World War produced; by the vast expansion of the mass
media of communication and especially the inclusion of Britain
within a European television network; by the new habit of holiday-
ing abroad; by the widespread showing of foreign films; by the

internationalization of government and of the machinery of economic control; by a massive expansion of foreign trade; and not least, by a rise in the general level of education, which has turned people towards a more international outlook' (1965:171-2). As a consequence of the new demands, both organizational patterns in the school system and teaching principles and methods have undergone and are undergoing deep transformations.

On the university level, the teaching of linguistics, applied linguistics, and particular languages closely follows the standards and patterns used in America. Several universities, such as Essex, Leeds, York, Canterbury and Warwick, are good examples. Some emphasize more the practical preparation of teachers for classroom work, like the Division of Modern Language Teaching in the London Institute of Education; others stress typically linguistic theory, like the School of Applied Linguistics at the University of Edinburgh.[4]

Another major change is a sudden, explosive development of foreign-language teaching in the primary schools, to children between the ages of seven and twelve. In 1961, there were perhaps twenty or thirty primary-school children in the whole country learning a foreign language (mainly French); the Department of Education and Science estimates that by 1967 the number will reach 100,000. The training of temporary teachers and the preparation of suitable materials have been undertaken jointly by the Department of Education and the Nuffield Foundation.

Organizations, official or private, like Her Majesty's Inspectors for Modern Languages, the Nuffield Foundation, the National Committee on Research and Development in Modern Languages, the British Council, the English-Teaching Information Centre, the British Linguistics Association, the Audio-Visual Languages Association, the Modern Language Association, etc., are contributing greatly to a rapid renovation in curricula and methods.

From the strictly methodological viewpoint, it must be said that the impact of linguistics in Britain has been similar to the one in America. The British school of linguistics has evolved within the past few years. General and applied linguistics are taught in several universities. In actual teaching, emphasis is placed on the spoken language as the first aim; the use of audio-visual equipment is developing and spreading, and, though more slowly, the use of language laboratories is increasing; television is the subject of educational experimentation; scientific research is gradually speeding up.

But it should be noted that the English teacher lays great importance on eye-contact with the student, on his personal presence in the classroom, on 'situational teaching'. 'Perhaps', Strevens remarks, 'for the reason that they are 'decontextualized'—out of situation—we have never accorded a major place to intensive drills and pattern practice. We do include them, of course, but not to the extent that American courses do. This idea that all language should be taught in a meaningful context is not new, but its acceptance in foreign language teaching is a rather recent trend' (1965:178).

France[5]

France has had the same vicissitudes in the history of foreign language teaching as most of the European countries. There were a few inspired attempts by individual teachers, while most teachers, inadequately prepared or untrained, continued in their conventional routine. But apart from a glorious past in the field of historical linguistics and experimental phonetics (the name of Abbé Rousselot is widely remembered), it is only in more recent years that applied linguistics and the methodology of foreign-language teaching have taken great strides. The deep changes and the rapid development that have taken place in the last fifteen years are due mainly to the establishment of efficient organized bodies of research and dissemination of information. These organizations, like the Alliance Française, the CREDIF and the BELC, have been so decisive and influential that they deserve fuller attention.

While the Alliance Française is mainly devoted to such practical purposes as teaching French to foreigners, the CREDIF (Centre de Recherches et d'Études pour la Diffusion du Français) and the BELC (Bureau pour l'Enseignement de la Langue et de la Civilisation Françaises a l'Étranger) have wider scopes and more scientific aims. They are both research centers which specialize in the teaching of French as a foreign language. Both prepare books, films, and other materials for teaching. Their information centers make available the results of their own work, such as aptitude and achievement tests. All materials are tested and evaluated both in and outside France. In addition, BELC maintains a library of 6000 volumes and 150 periodicals.

CREDIF and BELC differ, however, in their specific activities and tend to complement each other's work. CREDIF, for example, has concentrated more on studies of modern French while

BELC has done more work in contrastive studies. BELC has done contrastive phonological studies comparing the phonology of French with that of English, Spanish, Italian, Arabic, and other modern languages. CREDIF has explored the problems of audio-visual aids and has equipped centers with audio-visual equipment. From CREDIF's work have come the two series of materials, Voix et images de France and Bonjour Line. BELC, on the other hand, has investigated the conditions of teaching French in different countries and has published materials such as Dialogues Africains.

It is easy to understand how the teaching of foreign languages as well as the teaching of French as a foreign language has evolved and reached very high standards during the past few years. Organized and enlightened efforts have worked the miracle. More recent events promise further growth.

One new reform project concerns the teaching of English at the university level. It envisages less emphasis on literature, more on linguistic knowledge and the mastery of the language itself.

Language laboratories have been introduced at the university level where English is the most frequent language taught. Oral tests administered in language labs have been introduced in higher schools like the École des Hautes Études Commerciales, the École des Mines and the École Polytechnique. According to a survey conducted by the Institut Pédagogique National in 1965, a rapid increase in the establishment of language laboratories is noticeable: from 2 in 1959 to 9 in 1960, 11 in 1961, 22 in 1962, 61 in 1963, and 116 in 1965!

Foreign language teaching is spreading also in elementary schools. In 1965-66, for the first time in France, an experiment in the teaching of English to primary school children was initiated under the sponsorship of the National Ministry of Education.

Applied Linguistics as it is commonly understood in Britain and the USA is gaining acceptance in France. Universities such as Besançon, Nancy, Strasburg, Paris, Grenoble have given academic recognition to this discipline. The University of Grenoble grants a Certificat de Linguistique Appliquée. The French Association of Applied Linguistics, founded in 1965, counts over 200 members and organized the first European linguistic institute, the Séminaire Européen de Linguistique Générale et Appliquée, after the fashion of the American summer institutes, at Besançon, Grenoble, and Nancy, with internationally known lecturers participating.

Progress in the basic concepts of modern methodology is also noticeable in the change in scope of the activities promoted by BEL. On January 1, 1966, BEL became BELC, a specialized section of the Centre International d'Études Pédagogiques of Sèvres, by the merging of BEL with SERPED (Service d'Étude et de Recherche pour les Pays en voie de Developpement) and CREC (Centre de Recherche pour l'Enseignement de la Civilisation).

No doubt this improved coordination of efforts will result in greater progress in foreign language teaching.

Germany[6]

German scholars and educators contributed their share to the renewal of methods of teaching modern languages: the name of Viëtor, among others, will be remembered. Some professional associations have also done their best to keep and spread the new ideas during the first half of the present century. However, as in other countries, school teachers in Germany have been rather resistant to change. The situation has been improving only since the 1950's.

The present progress has been stimulated above all by the action of a few research centers: the Unesco-Institut für Pädagogik in Hamburg has promoted international Conferences on foreign language teaching to primary school children; the Pädagogisches Zentrum in Berlin has been sponsoring and organizing very successful international conventions on modern methods of foreign-language teaching; and as a permanent institution specifically concerned with language teaching, the Sprachkybernetisches Forschungszentrum at Heidelberg has been especially active. This one deserves special mention.[7]

Reaction to modern second language learning methods is still diffuse and continues to lack concerted official support. No chairs for applied linguistics or kindred subjects have been created at Universities though at Giessen University a lecturer for French didactics has just been appointed. Thus the Sprachkybernetisches Forschungszentrum at Heidelberg is still the only agency which is devoted to full-time work on new teaching methods in languages. As such it is gaining recognition in a gratifying manner, not least at Heidelberg University where the Professor of Education and again the Professor of Psychology are cooperating closely with the SKF on research projects (report by H. P. Walz).

Recent activities and achievements of the SKF have been

(1) The <u>International Review of Applied Linguistics</u> (IRAL). This review gathers contributions on a high academic level from all over the world.

(2) Documentation. The total number of catalog cards compiled from bibliographical data has now reached a figure of 7588 publications on modern second language teaching methods (including publications in relevant marginal fields of study). To make specialized literature more easily accessible, a temporary system of descriptors has been developed. This comprises some 1200 classified terms and contains a number of references and cross references. To facilitate the use of electronic media (punchcard systems, computers, etc.), all publications have been coded on the basis of a highly developed reference system. To make maximum use of the documentation department more feasible, all publications are excerpted and 1286 such excerpts are now available. In addition, 676 abstracts have been compiled and furnished with descriptors and code numbers. All excerpts and abstracts are recorded on punch tapes. Systematic storing of information on language teaching machines and other technical data has now reached some 900 items.

(3) Foreign Language Achievement Testing. A battery of English tests has been developed to ascertain as comprehensively as possible the knowledge of English brought to the University by students fresh from secondary school. The same battery has been applied to another set of students after their second and again after their third year at the Dolmetscher-Institut of Heidelberg University. The purpose of these tests is to derive a reasonably reliable indication of the effectiveness of foreign language teaching in German secondary schools, and again the effectiveness of language teaching on the university level. Similar tests for French, Russian, and other languages are planned.

(4) Language Aptitude Test. The SKF, in cooperation with Paul Pimsleur, is at present engaged in developing a language aptitude test to suit German conditions.

(5) Language Laboratory Experiment in German secondary schools. A detailed investigation of the reactions of German school children to language laboratory methods was conducted over a period of more than six months with about 100 school pupils of various ages. The purpose of the investigation was not to establish the usefulness of language laboratory work over against traditional methods, but to record the children's reactions in view of their individual characteristics.

(6) Audio-oral Correspondence Courses. Teaching through postal transmission of tape recorded language instruction was first tried on fifteen adults in various professions who had no previous knowledge of French but were taught enough French to permit their active participation in a seminar on worker priests in Paris. The methods employed proved very successful. The success of the pilot course encouraged the Volkswagen Foundation to finance similar courses in other languages, including modern Hebrew. The method will probably also be employed in the mass instruction of German elementary-school teachers, several thousand of whom need instruction in elementary English. The plan is to develop rapidly a teaching and counseling organization which will simultaneously comprise between 1000 and 2000 such teachers.

Other activities being developed by the Center are teacher training, an international seminar on foreign language teaching, linguistic instruction of Peace Corps workers, investigation of the linguistic training of migrant workers in Germany, a model course for German youths who want to go to France, textbook adaptation, etc.

Other countries are developing similar programs in different degrees. For many countries, available documentation is still regrettably inadequate. However, some can be mentioned.

Canada[8]

Canada is one of the countries where linguistic problems, mainly occasioned by a bilingual situation, have received and are receiving more up-to-date solutions. A number of textbooks and techniques, which might be grouped under the heading of 'improved direct method', have been developed lately. Oral work preceding writing, use of audio-visual aids and illustrated texts, pattern drills, etc., are the chief characteristics of this eclectic methodology, where the teacher remains the director of classroom learning. Foreign language teaching, on an experimental basis, has been more successful so far on the primary school level than in the secondary schools which are still hampered by old-fashioned examinations. Some centers, like the Department of Modern Languages at the Université Laval in Québec, are well organized research centers with the most modern equipment and well prepared staff. The work of Prof. W. F. Mackey at this university is of unique value in the field of language teaching methodology. (See bibliography.)

Italy

In Italy, two main trends have characterized the reform of foreign language teaching methods: the training of teachers on the secondary school level, and the dissemination of the new ideas about applied linguistics. The former program has been carried out through a number of refresher courses organized by the government-sponsored Centro Didattico per la Scuola Media (Center for the organization of pedagogical development on the lower secondary-school level) and through a special program of Cornell University (with aid from the Ford Foundation) for teachers of English in the technical schools. The latter program has developed mainly by means of conferences and publications. The Italian Center for Applied Linguistics (CILA), founded in 1964, is developing a series of projects to disseminate information and to carry out experiments.

Spain

In Spain, the program for the establishment and expansion of departments of English in the leading universities is moving forward with a recent grant from the Ford Foundation to Georgetown University for cooperation and support. Under the program, electronic language laboratories are being installed in approximately five Spanish universities where departments of English have been established, or will be soon. Since, in general, the teaching of English in the universities has not hardened into a fixed tradition, the program will permit the teaching of oral English and other courses in the five-year university curriculum and the demonstration of audio-visual-lingual techniques in modern methodology of language teaching.

Holland

In Holland, experimentation is under way on the use of language laboratories in secondary schools. Of particular interest are the two 'electronic classrooms' used at St. Ignatius' school at Amsterdam. (Cf. Mooijman in Libbish 1964: 54-65.)

Philippine Islands

Finally, among the programs going on in the Far East, the Philippine-University of California Language Program might be mentioned. A published report by Clifford H. Prator, Language Teaching in the Philippines (1950), was the stimulus for the proposal to develop a Philippine language program to meet the requirements of the nation in its relation to the rest of the world. A general plan that has been under way since 1957 involves the following lines of work: (1) the in-service and pre-service training of teachers in the Philippines, (2) the training of second language specialists both in the Philippines and in the United States, (3) the production of instructional materials, and (4) research and experimental projects. The institutions responsible for this far-reaching program have been UCLA and the PCLS (Philippine Center for Language Study, established in Manila in 1957). A large part of this work has been carried out or is in progress. Any reader of the 1965 Report will be impressed by how much methodological and linguistic research has been accomplished. Problems of bilingualism (English on one side and Tagalog, Pangasinan, Cebuano on the other) have been particularly investigated with rigorously scientific method and on a large population scale. (Cf. The Philippine Center for Language Study, Philippine-University of California Language Program. A report of its eight years of operation, 1957-65.)

Classification of Methods

Up to this point the situation in the field of language-teaching methodology has been considered from a geographical standpoint. The above survey can be usefully supplemented with a vertical stratification of old and new methods in use within the above geographical areas. Although newer trends in teaching have been generally accepted, the older ones have not disappeared. But it is possible to speak of certain prevailing trends: (1) a tendency toward the integration of multiple features into an eclectic type of methodology, and (2) the growing interest in experimental research applied to language teaching procedures.

The following tentative classification of methods may be offered.

(1) The formal approach

What has been called the 'classical' or 'traditional' method is usually just a conventional routine devoid of theoretical background and based on the experience or on the so-called 'common sense' of the individual teacher. It is not really 'classical'; this would imply reference to an ideal standard, whereas this routine is entirely worthless. Nor is it really 'traditional', for this pre-supposes a long-standing acceptance, whereas this practice dates back only to the beginning of the past century. The formal approach includes those varieties of teaching procedures that proceed from the abstract study of grammar rules to their application through translation. Its character of 'formalism' depends, therefore, on the practice of abstracting from the concrete living language, while submitting it to conceptual anatomy. It may also be called an 'informative approach' (I. Morris), because it tends to impart knowledge or information about the language without caring about the practical mastery of the language. Such an approach, not really concerned with the living language, makes no attempt to teach pronunciation beyond an introductory lesson or two in which the foreign speech sounds are roughly equated with those of the learner's native language (the a of padre as in father).

The formal approach finds its application mainly in two methods. The 'grammar-translation method' is the more detached from actual language, being concerned only with the general rules that govern the written language and basing practice exclusively on the exercise of translation from and into the foreign language. The 'reading method' deals with the language itself, but it gives excessive consideration, time, and effort to decoding the written language on the basis of grammar and analytic translation. Therefore, most of the criticisms leveled against the former also apply to the latter.

It would be rather easy to refute the formal methods, for 'from their fruits ye shall judge them'. There is abundant evidence accumulated through over a century of teaching that such methods cannot produce any complete mastery of the language. However, a more detailed critique might not be entirely inappropriate, since the 'method-consciousness' of many language teachers demands a thorough evaluation of all approaches.

Although this approach may be the easiest way to teach a language, it is the most ineffective and unscientific way to learn a language. A few remarks may suffice to prove the point.

Usually no selection is made of practical or useful linguistic materials to be incorporated in the texts. The beginning lessons may be designed to train the students to read the classics in the foreign language by including archaic words, rare literary expressions, and stylistic tricks. Lack of selection and gradation will result in an amount and a complexity of structure and vocabulary that puzzles the student and kills his motivation from the very beginning.

The way the vocabulary is taught usually presents special difficulties to the beginner. First, no scientific choice of words is made, based on frequency counts, cognates, or practical utility. The words that happen to be in the selection from the classics, or which are used in sentences to illustrate the grammatical rules, are listed and supposed to be memorized as individual units, or even worse, they are met and dropped from memory on account of their excessive number. Second, the teaching procedure is inadequate. Sometimes as many as 35 new words may be given in one lesson. No attempt is made to recall and drill these words in the following lessons; and teaching them in lists without any context makes retention almost impossible. No wonder the student feels lost in a welter of unclassified material.

Nor does the teaching of grammar fare any better —although it is supposed to be the strong point of the method. Generally it is traditional grammar derived from Latin and based on unscientific and artificial rules and classifications which are not applicable to modern languages. Grammar is taught abstractly, analytically, and deductively, even to young students who are still insecure in the logical processes of abstraction and deduction. As a consequence, no transfer of training takes place between theory and practice, for this transfer demands the incorporation of rules into automatic patterns operating at the peripheral level of language encoding and decoding, not at a deeper, conscious level.

In conclusion, there is no possible justification, whether theoretical or practical, for adopting the formal approach, even if it be granted that a mere reading knowledge of the foreign language may become a valid objective of instruction. The formal methods do not teach the language itself, but teach about the language, generally by perpetuating traditional fallacies and presenting numerous pitfalls. They are not at all useful for learning the spoken language, and hardly justifiable for teaching the written language. A strictly theoretical grammatical method can be accepted only on a very advanced level, with students who already have a good practical mastery of the language.

(2) The functional approach

The role of any functional method is the practical one of leading to the mastery of the living language, especially in its oral form. Most procedures are functionally oriented toward bringing the learner into direct contact with the oral language. The functional character lies in the aim of these methods —to have the student handle the language directly and master it in meaningful communication situations. The classification suggested below is based on the specific emphasis placed by each of the different methods on certain particular features of the language learning process.

(a) The Direct Methods

The qualification of 'directness' implies an immediate contact between the learner and the foreign language without either the intermediary of the learner's own language or any grammatical theory. The following are some 'direct methods':

The Berlitz Method. This is certainly one of the earliest and most publicized examples of the direct method. Maximilian Berlitz (born in Poland in 1852) founded his first school in New York City with the practical purpose of teaching the basic tools for oral communication. This explains the exclusive stress on the oral form of the language. Some of the salient characteristics are universally known. The teachers are native speakers of the language. Instruction is either individual or directed to small classes (never more than ten pupils).

The two main principles of the Berlitz Method are (1) direct association of the foreign speech with the learner's thought: he must learn as soon as possible to 'think in the foreign language'; and (2) constant use of the foreign language without ever using the learner's own language. (Berlitz 1949: 3).

Consequently, concrete vocabulary is taught through object lessons. Abstract words are taught by association of ideas. Grammar is conveyed to the pupil merely by example and visual demonstration. The first step is always oral, based on listening and repeating. Words are always presented in sentences, like 'What's this?'—'It's a pencil.' The oral drill requires that the native teacher be a fluent and correct speaker, the classes small, and a great deal of class work be devoted to it from the beginning (at least five hours a week).

The following points are suggested by the Berlitz School:[9]

Oral Procedure
Never translate: demonstrate.
Never explain: act.
Never make a speech: ask questions.
Never imitate mistakes: correct.
Never speak with single words: use sentences.

43165

Never speak too much: make students speak much.
Never use the book: use your lesson plan.
Never jump around: follow your plan.
Never go too fast: keep the pace of the student.
Never speak too slowly: speak normally.
Never speak too quickly: speak naturally.
Never speak too loudly: speak naturally.
Never be impatient: take it easy.

Reading Procedure

Student reads aloud; teacher corrects mistakes, then has
   student repeat entire sentence.
Upon completion of the lesson, teacher asks five questions;
   student answers.
Student then asks five (or more) questions on the lesson and
   teacher answers. [10]

In sum, the Berlitz Method tolerates no use of the native language, no translation, no grammar rules; reading and writing
should come only after the student has attained mastery of speech.

From a positive standpoint the Berlitz Method represents a
great advance over the formal methods by placing a great emphasis on drill in aural understanding and speaking. A good foundation in the spoken language makes subsequent learning of reading
and writing easier and more thorough. And special attention is
accorded the psychological aspects of teaching. [11]

The dangers, I believe, are more on the part of the uncautious
teacher than on the part of the method itself. The teacher may
sometimes waste time by not using the learner's language when
useful and advisable. He may overemphasize the concrete by
sticking to concrete material, which of course is the only kind
directly demonstrable. He can fail to grade the language material properly, overstressing the principle of visual demonstrabil-
ity, for demonstrable material may not always be the easiest in
pronunciation or grammatical form. Finally, the teacher, by
using conversation as a dominant form of teaching, may unwittingly
present many different forms for the same idea.

It is undoubtedly possible, however, for the Berlitz Method to
avoid these pitfalls by a careful selection and gradation of the
language material and by imparting to the Berlitz teacher a sense
of moderation. [12]

The Eclectic Direct Method. This is usually associated with a
group of British teaching experts who worked chiefly on the

teaching of English as a foreign language largely in the Orient and lately in Britain. Among the more commonly known are Harold E. Palmer (see Chapter 6), Michael West, Lawrence Faucett, H. B. Drake, I. Morris, J. O. Gauntlett. (See bibliography for works.) Even though this methodological concept was largely based on the results of practical experience, it still included some scientific characteristics such as a more accurate analysis of the linguistic material and the consideration of some suggestions from educational psychology. It is owing to the efforts of these teachers that progress in foreign-language teaching could be made during the years 1920-35.[13]

Their work was carried on mainly in the three areas of pronunciation, vocabulary, and grammar. Of course, the pronunciation material used in their textbooks was prepared before the recent work (of Pike and of Smith and Trager) on the application of phonemics to the teaching of foreign languages. Using Daniel Jones's analysis of English phonetics as a foundation, these teachers worked out explanations, drills on special difficulties for different language groups, pronouncing dictionaries, phonograph records, and so forth. (Cf. Jones in bibliography.) Some pronunciation drills, such as Faucett's, can still be useful in ordinary practice, but the system of marking regular English spelling for pronunciation, invented by Sir William Craigie, seems too elaborate to be practical in teaching. It is also known how useful Palmer's work on intonation has been.

Second, basing their teaching mostly on reading, these methodologists carefully selected and graded vocabulary materials according to frequency and usefulness. Word counts and limited and functional vocabularies were then prepared for this purpose,[14] and reading books were compiled within these vocabularies.[15] The same principle was followed in building conversation courses.

Third, grammar was brought back to the classroom. These men, unlike the pure 'direct-methodologists', recognized the usefulness and even the necessity of presenting some sort of grammar to their pupils for more effective learning of the language. But it was no longer the old traditional and formal grammar, which had caused difficulties for many teachers and students of foreign languages. They did a great deal of work on the analysis of the language, in this case English, from a functional point of view; this is what they called 'living English grammar', which meant a thorough drilling of the structures in current usage.[16]

The success attained by these methodologists was remarkable and was due largely to well prepared teachers and good textbooks.[1]

But the application of a not scientifically validated type of linguistics, ignorance of phonemics, grammar analyzed promiscuously
both through meaning and form, occasional exaggeration in
teaching conversation without insisting enough on basic patterns,
represent some weaknesses in the method that may impair its
efficiency.

This trend, with some improvements from modern linguistics,
is still followed in some British universities today. [18]

The Simplification Methods. [19] These methods are based on a
limitation and selection of lexical and structural items in order
to ensure a rapid and substantial mastery of the essentials of the
language. Under this category two forms of teaching methods can
be included: Basic English and the Graded-Direct Method.

Basic English. [20] The prominent aspect of Basic English is the
limitation of the English vocabulary to a body of 850 words.
These can be made to express many meanings by proper combination. [21]

Basic English claims to have three uses: (1) as a possible
language; (2) as a means of simplifying and clarifying obscure or
elaborate English prose or poetry, or as a means of translating
from foreign languages into English; (3) as a method of teaching
English as a foreign language. The third objective seems to be
the most common so far.

Basic English has also developed a few practical procedures of
teaching. Nothing new, indeed, has been added to the teaching of
pronunciation, which is conveyed by the usual imitation and description of sounds, based on Jones's analysis. But in teaching
vocabulary and grammar, the learner's language can be used.
An interesting point is that words and structures are supposed to
be introduced according to carefully regulated steps, and words
are always to be presented in structures. To get an idea of how
Basic reduces linguistic material, we need only notice that its
system uses only 16 verbs (be, come, do, get, give, go, have,
keep, let, make, put, take, say, see, send, seem) and two auxilia-
ries (will, may, plus the auxiliary use of be, have, and do).

The method makes use of a wide range of reading material for
further practice. When transition from Basic to full English is
called for, the new vocabulary needed is found naturally in the
readings and is explained by a General Basic English Dictionary
which includes some 20,000 non-Basic words defined in Basic.

Undoubtedly Basic English has some merit. The material is
carefully selected according to a definite principle. The structures are presented according to the concrete categories of living

English, not according to traditional grammatical theory. There is some excellent reading material produced by a group of scholars who have been working consistently for about forty years.

There are also drawbacks. Pronunciation tends to be neglected and generally there is no planned series of oral drills. The selection criterion is not pedagogical but merely semantic. In other words, the intent is to give the capacity to express a great number of meanings with fewer words, rather than to learn expressions of high frequency and utility in ordinary English. This one-sidedness leads to special difficulties in the teaching of grammar and in the presentation of vocabulary.

It is true that the Basic English structures are very simple, but unless they are used properly by native speakers they are bound to sound awkward.

Similarly the vocabulary is only seemingly simplified, but in reality, since it is reckoned in terms of words rather than of lexical items or meanings, it inevitably contains many more than 850 semantic items. The verb to get, for example, has an immense variety of meanings, and consequently the foreign learner will be bewildered by its use in so many different contexts. The multiplicity of meanings derives also from the English habit of combining certain different prepositions with the same verb to convey different meanings. Thus, while for Basic English these common denominators seem particularly handy, they add confusion in the mind of the student. In such common cases as get back at, get on, get up, get behind, get out, get off, etc. there is probably a common semantic component, but it is not readily perceived by the beginning student. (Similar problems would arise in German if it were reduced to a similar basic system.) This difficulty is further complicated by the use of basic verbs in place of more specific verbs. The sentence He gave the ball a kick instead of He kicked the ball, —a circumlocution designed to avoid nonbasic verbs—is a clear illustration of how an attempt to simplify can turn into an odd complication.

A language, since it is a living organism, bears with it unavoidable redundancies and complications; trying to reduce these will tend to make the language artificial, awkward, and useless.

The Graded Direct Method.[22] This is a form of 'direct' method insofar as it aims at placing the student in direct contact with the foreign language without the intermediary of his native tongue so as to force him to think in the foreign language itself. It avoids, however, the wasteful spontaneity of the earlier direct methods in that it offers graded material. Besides a selected

vocabulary, the material is 'organized into graded sentence se-
quences, each building outward from the preceding ones—establishing in the students' minds the basic structure of the language,
and substituting the active mastery of meaning for mere rote
memory' (Richards 1952: 1).

A very important concept in the mind of Dr. Richards is what
he calls the SEN-SIT, or 'a unit made up of a sentence in the
situation which gives it meaning ... Teaching a language effectively consists of inventing, arranging, presenting, and testing
SEN-SITS ... When the structure of the sentence corresponds
to a structure easily perceived in the situation, the SEN-SIT is
said to be clear' (1947:1). Grading is therefore the distribution
of these SEN-SITS along a meaning scale from the least to the
most ambiguous. Intelligibility is the main grading criterion.
Once the SEN-SITS have been arranged in the ideal order of intelligibility, they are presented without recourse to the learner's
own language and by making use of ingenious pictures[23] and of
original audio-visual aids.

Grammar is taught by reducing all the material to a few basic
structures, introducing each structure in its right place in the
ideal meaningful order, and by substitution exercises ('teaching
the structures through changes in the variables' (Notes, p. 2).

Oral work is not neglected. The Graded-Direct Method 'leaves
the amount of attention invested in perfecting pronunciation quite
open, adjusted to the learner's probable needs, the school situation, resources, etc. ';[24] the textbooks themselves, however,
do not go into the question of phonetic training in any detail.[25]

Obviously, a method of this sort can be successful with learners of all ages. The use of concrete illustrative material, the
efficient limitation of the linguistic material, the grading designed
to do away with a great many learning difficulties, the clear and
realistic teaching of grammar, the excellent teaching material
tested through many years of experience—all are worthwhile
features. On the other hand, certain weaknesses can easily be
detected. There is too rigorous adherence to the principle of
monolingual instruction, while the native language could sometimes facilitate learning. As in Basic English, the reduction of
vocabulary can occasion awkward constructions or usages, both
lexical and grammatical, such as the following: 'What is the
time? The time is one.' 'He is giving a push to the door.' 'Mary
has a potato in her hand. She is taking the skin off with a knife.'
(Richards and Gibson 1952: 35, 59, 92). (Why not just use the
word peel here?) The trouble is that passing from Basic English

to regular English may entail much unlearning, if the student has to leave aside simplified, artificial constructions for more complicated, natural ones.

Despite these criticisms it cannot be denied that the Graded-Direct Method has enjoyed widespread success in the teaching of English, due mostly to its ingenious and original textbooks and audiovisual aids.

(b) The intensive method[26]

Beside commercial courses advertised in several countries, a more scientific version of the Intensive Method was developed under the Army Specialized Training Program. This seems to have been the most successful adaptation so far. Usually the teaching is carried on by a two-man 'team' composed of the linguist, who gives explanations on the structure of the language, and the instructor, assigned to the drilling sessions.

The intensive character of language study lies especially in that part of the work done with the instructor. The materials to be drilled and overlearned are presented in six basic steps:

Imitation. The new vocabulary is presented word for word. Each word is repeated twice for each student. After giving the new vocabulary, the complete sentence or parts of it, if necessary, are presented following the same procedure. Errors must be immediately corrected.

Repetition. The student will repeat twice, without a model, each sentence that he has learned.

Translation. The instructor gives the sentence and the student will give the English translation.

Rotation. The first sentence is given to the first student, the second to the second, and so on around the class. Then the first sentence is given to the second student, and so on successively, until all have begun with the first sentence.

Discontinuous repetition. Still paying attention to pronunciation and exact imitation of intonation, the instructor takes the sentences in random order, giving the sentence in the foreign language and then saying to the student, 'repeat' or 'translate'. Each student must take part, but no student should know what or when he is going to be asked.

Dialogue practice. Short but complete dialogues are used. The instructor begins the dialogue practice himself with the first student. Then the first student will have to repeat the dialogue with the second student, exchanging roles.

In addition, reviews at the beginning of each class hour and exercises for the last hours of the class are always used. The exercises commonly used are of the following types: illustrative (to establish a grammatical point), substitution, response, translation, variation, and replacement exercises.

Beside the scientifically conceived intensive language programs developed over the past twenty years by the Defense Language Institute, other programs characterized by maximum intensiveness have been advertised. Articles in nationally distributed periodicals have publicized experimental projects in the Washington area known as 'Total Immersion' and purporting to produce 'Instant Linguistics' or showing 'How to Learn a Language in Five Days'. As in the past, journalistic oversimplifications of language-learning programs give the public the impression that these 'new methods' could produce 'miracles' and imply that all other methods are wasteful of time and effort in comparison. There is the misleading implication that one can 'learn to speak a foreign language' in a few days, when in fact the results lead at best to a temporary collection of expedient cognates and glib uttering of unnatural or pat phrases rather than to spontaneous conversation as carried on by mature adults.

All intensive methods require a high degree of linguistic aptitude in the learner, a reduction of the language to basic forms, and sufficient time for practice. Intensiveness cannot do away with time, but it implies rather more time in less time. Intensive procedures are to be considered part of any good method of language teaching. But one caution needs voicing: such procedures should not produce stress and lead the student to frustration.[27]

(c) The audiovisual method[28]

As was shown in a previous chapter, the use of visual aids in language teaching dates back as far as Comenius and regained vigor at the end of the last century. But not until after the last war did technological aids have a deep impact on language teaching. Wall charts and printed illustrations have been surpassed, although not entirely replaced, by slides, motion pictures, TV programs, with the reinforcement of machines to reproduce sound like phonographs and tape recorders. Audiovisual aids have a pertinent role in foreign language teaching and have found in the language laboratory their most modern function. Simply mentioning all the achievements attained by the application of the new media and aids to language teaching would require several chapters.

What ought to be stressed, however, from a methodological standpoint, is that audiovisual techniques cannot alone constitute a 'method' but only a subsidiary part of any method which aims at teaching the spoken language. There is also the danger that, by relying solely on the machine, the learner may take on a rather passive attitude (listening, watching, and nothing more) thus jeopardizing the integrity of the goal of language learning— the ability to communicate actively in the foreign language, not just receive messages passively.

Therefore, the audiovisual way of teaching and learning can only improperly be called a 'method', although it represents one of the most valuable assets within the frame of any functional oral approach.

(d) The linguistic (-anthropological) method

The impact of modern linguistics on language teaching has been deep and far-reaching. Structural analysis of the language to be studied, scientific classification of its basic and typical features on the phonemic, morphological, syntactical, and seman- tic levels, analysis of contrasts between native language and target language, and other achievements of modern linguistic structural analysis have been tremendously influential in revo- lutionizing the methods of teaching foreign languages. Especially in the United States, the meeting between linguistics and language teaching constitutes a uniquely important chapter in the history of modern methodology.[29]

The linguistic dimension, consolidated with the anthropological, is only one basis of language teaching method, as H. E. Palmer had already clearly perceived and stated. It concerns only the objective aspect of language study, that is, the linguistic material to be analyzed, selected, graded, and presented to the student, while language teaching must take into account a number of other subjective and objective dimensions. There is, furthermore, no doubt that the linguistic model used in the analysis will affect the ease with which the student will assimilate the patterns of the lan- guage; in short, a theory of grammar is not altogether indifferent to language pedagogy.[30] But this only remotely refers to the teaching process. In the actual process of teaching the objective material has to be adapted to the particular student and to his ob- jectives.

All this is to say that the emphasis on the contributions of linguistics should not become exclusive nor dominant. There is no
such thing as a 'linguistic method' but only a linguistic component
of method.

(e) The audio-lingual (aural-oral) method

Insofar as only the audio-lingual aspect of language learning is
emphasized, this so-called 'method' is reduced to a set of procedures or techniques aiding the auditory assimilation and the
building of productive skills in the foreign language. Language is
sound, but it is not only sound. It is cultural content, ability to
read and write, appreciation of the literature, and so forth. It
is habit and conscious control, a set of automatized verbal habits
controlled by the awareness of how the language works. Therefore, it is improper to speak of a 'method' in this case: it is a
single, though very important, element of language acquisition.
No one will deny the tremendous impact of the audio-lingual
trend upon the whole methodology of foreign language teaching.
But its real value can be understood only when the audio-lingual
segment is placed in its right position within the total frame of
the language-learning process.
Recent theoretical and experimental studies on the validity of
the audio-lingual method indicate that it only partially fulfils the
requirements of foreign-language teaching. If taken narrowly,
it would overemphasize verbal automatization and neglect more
conscious operations required by human learning; it would be
reduced to a mere 'mim-mem' type of learning where mimicry
and memorization would exhaust all phases of language acquisition. [31]

(3) The integrated approach

Theory and experience converge to show that the complexity
of the teaching process can be met only with adaptable, flexible,
manysided procedures. Overemphasis on one or a few aspects
of the process of language acquisition has been responsible for
the present proliferation of methods, each one claiming almost
absolute truth or unique value. Open-minded teachers and
scholars are convinced that no one single factor can explain and
guide language learning as a developmental process. A more
comprehensive philosophy of language learning, therefore, points
to the necessity of postulating a multidimensional approach and,

accordingly, of keeping methodological programming open to
new adaptations and contributions from various provinces of
theory and experience.

Integration of a multiplicity of procedures into the same
method can be based merely on experiential or prescientific
grounds or on truly scientific premises and criteria. In the
former case, we have a 'functional eclectic methodology' which
is open to all valuable suggestions from systematic experience
or even from science, but is not in itself a strictly scientific
construction. In the latter case, integration is the result of a
scientific process and we have a 'scientific integrated approach'.

H. E. Palmer termed his own methodology a 'multiple line
of approach' as based on an eclectic attitude. 'This complete
method, he declares ... boldly incorporates what is valuable in
any system or method of teaching and refuses to recognize any
conflict, except the conflict between the good and the inherently
bad. The complete method will embody every type of teaching
except bad teaching, and every process of learning except defec-
tive learning. The complete method (of which the multiple line
of approach is the expression) is the antithesis of the special or
patent method. Patent or proprietary methods very often, but
not always, resemble patent medicines. We know what they are.
A patent language method, like a patent medicine, claims to pre-
vent or to cure all possible ills (linguistic or physical, as the
case may be) by repeated applications of one special device or
drug; both of them claim to kill innumerable birds with one
stone' (1964:110-11). On the contrary, the eclectic approach will
say, 'Find the right stone to kill the right bird', and 'It is often
advisable to kill one bird with more than one stone'. 'This principle, which underlies all others, leaves the door open for new
devices, new methods, and improvements on the old ones. It
leaves us free to welcome and to adopt all sorts of innovations,
provided such innovations are likely to prove of value' (1964:114).
The practical eclecticism advocated by Palmer is not unscientific,
for it is particularly inclined to welcome the best contributions
from science—linguistics or anthropology, psychology or neuro-
physiology, etc. However, the whole approach is nothing more
than a general attitude without real theoretical organization. It
does not constitute a 'system'.

The present author therefore feels the need of going further
along the line of integration in order to establish a genuinely
'scientific integrated methodology'. In order to banish whatever
is arbitrary and onesided, there seems to be no other way than

exploring more deeply and extensively the process of language learning on the basis of an interdisciplinary scientific approach. The need for multiple-disciplinary and interdisciplinary support arises from the very nature of language, which in its ontological complexity can be adequately studied only by several converging scientific disciplines.[32] Such scientific multidimensionality stems from the complexity of the factors at work within the individual learner and his existential situation. Therefore, a truly scientific approach has to consider and to base its principles on linguistics, on the objective side of learning, and psychology, on the subjective side, and on several sciences that can clarify the various aspects and factors in the learning situation. Any method stemming from a scientific integrated approach ought to be derived from (1) a scientific linguistic and anthropological analysis of language in general and of the specific language to be taught, (2) a psycholinguistic analysis of the process of second-language learning, (3) a definition of the specific objectives to be attained by a particular course of language study, and (4) the results of both a general theory of teaching experience and experimentation in foreign-language teaching (historical and experimental dimensions). Granted the theoretical validity of such a model as afforded by an interdisciplinary approach, all integrated methods and procedures, to be actually valid and effective, will have to be tested through experimental research.[33] This, I believe, is the only way to real progress in language teaching.

Conclusion

Language teaching seems to be following two significant directions. Linguistic teachers and scholars are sharing a growing feeling that effective language teaching needs to be based on the consideration of many factors and aspects. In the near future, indeed, already in many circles today, talking about the 'grammar-translation method' or the 'audio-lingual method' no longer will make any sense, since they will be envisaged as only partial sets of principles and procedures to be integrated in a larger methodological framework (methodological integration).

The definitive value of a method will have to be established by careful scientific experimentation. Experimental research in foreign-language teaching in the past twenty years has accumulated an immense body of material and results and is gradually taking on greater significance. But few conclusions based on such research have as yet attained a high degree of probability; many procedural issues are awaiting appropriate solutions; design-making is particularly difficult in experimenting on teaching; and adequate models of effective teaching are still a desideratum. [34] However, interdisciplinary programming under the joint responsibility of linguists, anthropologists, psychologists, neurologists, statisticians, and interested teachers, is the indispensable guarantee for success in future attempts at improving foreign-language teaching.

NOTES

[1] Documentation about the first twenty years of methodological development in the United States can be found especially in the following summaries: Moulton (1961); Walsh, Donald D., The Teaching of Modern Foreign Languages in the United States, in Libbish (1964:85-90); Stack, Edward M., Advances in Language Teaching in the United States, in Libbish (1964:66-82).

[2] A detailed bibliography for the period between 1940 and 1960 can be found in Moulton (1961:90-109).

[3] Recent documentation on the British situation can be found, besides the pamphlets issued by Her Majesty's Stationery Office and some survey books published by the Modern Language Association and by the Incorporated Association of Assistant Masters, in the following publications: Bearman (91-98); Dash (99-109); Ewing (110-22); all in Libbish (1964); Strevens (1965).

[4] These impressions agree with what the author learned on visits to the two universities of London and Edinburgh.

[5] The more recent information is taken from a series of publications by the Council of Europe, like Développements récents dans le domaine de l'enseignement des langues vivantes (Strasbourg: Conseil de l'Europe, 1964), and from unpublished reports issued by the BEL and the CREDIF.

[6] Some items of the present paragraph depend on information gathered by this writer through his direct participation in programs of the German language centers.

[7] Information about the SKF is to be found in an unpublished report presented by the Director, Prof. H. P. Walz, to the International Conference on Second Language Problems organized by the CAL (Washington, D. C.) and the BELC (Paris) at Quebec, Canada, April 20-23, 1966.

[8] Cf. Jeanes, R. W., Recent Advances in Modern Language Teaching in Canada, in Libbish (1964:35-53).

9 From unpublished material kindly communicated by the Berlitz School in Washington, D. C.

10 The student reads only material already drilled orally.

11 Cf. the psychological or personality qualifications of a 'Berlitz professor'. (Unpublished notes of the Berlitz School).

12 Cf. Berlitz Method (New York: Berlitz School of Languages Publications); Berlitz English, Books I, II (1949); Berlitz Business English (1949); Berlitz Idiom and Grammar (1949); Berlitz English for Children (1949); Berlitz English Literature (1949), etc. Similar books have been prepared for other languages.

13 It is true that methodological treatises and textbooks produced by these experts were directly concerned with the teaching of English as a foreign language to students of Eastern countries. However, many of their principles could be, and were, easily applied to the teaching of other modern languages.

14 Cf. West (1936 and 1953). Cf. also West and Bannerjee (1936).

15 Cf. e.g. the Oxford English Series.

16 Cf. Palmer and Blandford (1950); Gratten and Gurrey (1929); and, with a more modern slant, Allen (1948).

17 Many of these textbooks are still effectively used in the Orient.

18 The present writer noticed this orientation in the London Institute of Education, Division of Modern Language Teaching, and in the Faculty of Education, University of Southampton, when visiting there in 1960.

19 This term is taken from Cochran (1958, chapter 5).

20 Cf. Ogden in bibliography. There exists a Basic English Foundation (117 Piccadilly, London).

21 As a proof of this, translations have been made of all types of materials into Basic, from the strictest technical books to the Basic Bible and to E. A. Poe's The Gold Bug (in Basic, the Gold Insect).

22 The method was originated by Dr. I. A. Richards and Miss Christine M. Gibson and is being followed and developed at Language Research Inc., 13 Kirkland Street, Cambridge, Mass. For documentation on the method see esp. Richards in bibliography.

23 Cf. English through Pictures (1952), a textbook using stick figure cartoons to present the SEN-SITS in the ideal order. The introduction appears translated into 41 languages, two Workbooks accompanying it for the use of the student, and a Teacher's Manual.

[24] Personal communication from Dr. Richards to Anne Cochran (1958:34).

[25] When the teacher is not a native speaker of English, the G.-D. Method offers special mechanical aids developed by Language Research, Inc.: stick figure cartoons, filmstrips, recordings, and lately sound-film-loops. The long filmstrips were broken up into lesson-loops. A lesson-loop consists of a 'length of 16 mm film, spliced head to tail to permit continuous running, the time for the complete cycle averaging two minutes'. (Richards 1952: 4). This type of loop 'attached to a standard projector, makes it possible to run short loops of sound-film continuously without re-threading'. (1952:3). It is easy to imagine how many interesting class drills, tests, and other exercises can be carried out by such a device.

[26] Cf. Moulton (1961); Angiolillo (1947); and unpublished documents of the Defense Language Institute (DLI).

[27] This warning has been reiterated by other authors: 'Our analysis ... militates against the adoption and use of teaching methodology employing extreme massing of practice and stress in the teaching process for foreign language learning'. Rocklyn and Montague (1965:1).

[28] The bibliography on this subject both in America and in Europe is enormous. It may be noted, however, that the so-called 'méthode audiovisuelle' has received wide attention especially in Europe, and in France it has been considerably developed by the experts of the CREDIF and BELC (Paris). Besides the reports circulated by these two institutions, one can refer to the following publication: Council of Europe (1964b). In the United States the insistence has been especially on the audio side of the learning process. This is one reason that explains the rapid and widespread use of the language laboratory on all school and university levels.

[29] Scores of articles have been written, especially in the U.S., about the contribution of linguistics to language teaching. It would be impossible to present here even a selected bibliography. An outstanding example of a linguistically oriented course is Fries (1945). Bloomfield's Outline Guide, already mentioned, is one of the most typical examples of a linguistics-oriented methodology, in the strict sense assigned the term in the phrase 'applied linguistics'.

[30] Cf. DiPietro (1966).

[31] Much has been said about the psychological weakness of the audio-lingual method by W. M. Rivers (1964): her book is a

rather negative summary of the limitations of such methodology. On an experimental basis, the comparison between the grammar-translation and audio-lingual methods has been made and reported by a linguist and a psychologist, G.A.C. Scherer and M. Wertheimer (1964): differences in the results depend on the respective different emphases. This is a further proof of the one-sidedness of both methods. The position of the Soviet methodologist, Belyayev, who stresses what he calls a 'conscious-practical method' is acceptable. (Cf. Belyayev (1963).

[32] This thesis is favored by Lado (1964) and Titone (1965).

[33] Cf. Gage (1964).

[34] Cf. Nostrand (1965). National Defense Language Development Program (1965 ff.). Center for Research on Language and Language Behavior, LLBA. (Ann Arbor: University of Michigan). British Council, English Teaching Information Centre, Language Teaching Abstracts (periodical, London). Center for Applied Linguistics, The Linguistic Reporter (periodical, Washington, D. C.). Cf. also the following summaries: Carroll (1961); reprinted in Gage (1964). Id. (1966), Lado and Ornstein (1967), Stern (1965).

REFERENCES

Ahn, Franz i. e. Johann Franz. 1834. Praktischer Lehrgang zur schnellen und leichten Erlernung der französischen Sprache. Von d. F. Ahns Zweiter cursus. 10 Aufl. Köln, M. Du Mont-Schauberg, 1847.

Allen, W. S. 1948. Living English structure. London, Longmans.

Angiolillo, P. F. 1947. Armed Forces' foreign language teaching: critical evaluation and implications. New York, Vanni.

Bagster-Collins, E. W. 1930. The history of modern language teaching in the United States. Reprinted from Studies in modern language teaching, vol. XVII, Publications of the American and Canadian committees on modern languages. New York, Macmillan.

Bahlsen, Leopold. 1905. The teaching of modern languages, transl. by M. Blackmore Evans. Boston, Ginn.

Bannerjee, N. W. and H. C. 1952. New Method English series. 8 vols.

Bearman, E. C. 1964. Progress and problems in modern language teaching. Advances in the teaching of modern languages, ed. by R. Libbish. 91-98. London, Pergamon and New York, McMillan.

Belyayev, B. V. 1963. The psychology of teaching foreign languages. Oxford, Pergamon Press.

Berlitz, Maximilian D. 1949. Illustrated book for children: how to use this book. New York, Berlitz Publications.

Blancke, Wilton W. 1939. General language as a prognosis of success in foreign language study. German quarterly 12:71-80.

Boethlingk, O. 1887. Pāṇinis Grammatik, herausgegeben, übersetzt erläutert und mit verschiedenen Indices versehen. Leipzig.

Bohl, Hermann. 1928. Der Bildungswert fremder Kulturen. Die Erziehung, III.

Bohlen, Adolf. 1963. Methodik des neusprachlichen Unterrichts. Heidelberg, Quelle und Meyer.

Bongers, H. 1947. History and principles of vocabulary control. Wocopi, Woerden, Holland.

Brebner, M. 1898. The method of teaching languages in Germany. London.

Breymann and Steinmüller. 1895-1909. Die neusprachliche Reform-Literatur von 1876-1909: eine bibliographisch-kritische Übersicht. 4 vols. Leipzig.

Brunner, Helmut. 1957. Altägyptische Erziehung. Wiesbaden, Harrassowitz.

Buchanan, M. A. and E. D. MacPhee. 1928. Modern language instruction in Canada. University of Toronto Press.

Carroll, J. B. 1961. Research on teaching foreign languages. Ann Arbor, University of Michigan Press.

——. 1966. Research in foreign language teaching: the last five years. Northwest Conference Reports of the Working Committees, ed. by R. G. Mead, 12-42.

Closset, Francois. 1953. Didactique des langues vivantes. Brussels and Paris, Didier.

Cochran, Anne. 1958. Modern methods of teaching English as a foreign language. Washington, D. C., Educational Services.

Coleman, Algernon. 1929. The teaching of modern foreign languages in the United States. (Publications of the American and Canadian Committees on Modern Languages.) New York, Macmillan.

Collins, H. F. 1934. Yearbook of education, 1933-1937. 5 v. Ed. in Chief: 1933-36, Lord Eustace Percy. London, Evans Bros.

Comenius (Jan Amos Komenský). 1568. Didactica magna.

———. 1631. Janua linguarum reserata aurea.

Compayré, C. 1880. Histoire critique des doctrines de l'éducation en France depuis le XVI siècle. Vol. 2. Paris.

Corpus glossariorum latinorum. 1888 ff. Leipzig, Teubner.

Council of Europe. 1964a. Développements récents dans le domaine de l'enseignement des langues vivantes. Strasbourg.

Council of Europe. 1964b. Recherches et techniques nouvelles au service de l'enseignement des langues vivantes. Strasbourg.

Cubberly, Ellwood Patterson. 1920. Readings in the history of education. New York, Houghton Mifflin.

———. 1948. The history of education. New York: Houghton Mifflin.

Dash, F. L. 1964. Fifty years of progress in modern language teaching. Advances in the teaching of modern languages, ed. by R. Libbish, 99-109. London, Pergamon.

De Backer, Aug. and Al, and C. Sommervogel. 1890. Bibliothèque de la Compagnie de Jésus, Vol. 1. Brussels.

De Boisgermain, P. Luneau. 1783. Cours de langue italienne. Paris.

Delattre, Pierre. 1947. A technique of aural-oral approach. Report on a University of Oklahoma experiment in teaching French. French Review, 20:238-250, and 311-24.

De Radonvilliers, Claude-Francois Lysarde. 1768. De la manière d'apprendre les langues. Paris.

De Sauzé, E. B. 1929. The Cleveland plan for the teaching of modern languages. Philadelphia, Winston Co.

DiPietro, R. J. 1966. Operational and taxonomic models in language teaching. Paper read at TESOL Conference, New York City, March 19, 1966.

Doyle, Henry Grattan. 1937. George Ticknor. Modern Language Journal 22.

Drake, Henry Burgess. 1939-50. An approach to English literature for students abroad. 5 vols. London, Oxford University Press, G. Cumberlege [1939-50].

———. 1948. Second language learning. New York, Ginn & Co.

Escher, Erwin. 1919. Essay on the sources and the history of the direct method of teaching modern languages until its establishment

in France and Germany. University of Chicago unpublished
Master's thesis.

Ewing, N.R. 1964. Advances in teaching method. Advances in
the teaching of modern languages, ed. by R. Libbish, 110-122.
London, Pergamon.

Faucett, Lawrence. 1927. The teaching of English in the Far East.
New York, World Book Co.

———. 1934. Practical pronunciation helps. Shanghai, Commercial
Press.

Faucett, Lawrence, and Maki Itsu. 1932. A study of English word
values statistically determined from the latest extensive word
counts. Tokyo, Matsumura Shanshodo.

Faucett, Lawrence, F.G. French, and M.G.M. Faucett. Oxford
English course.

Franke, F. 1896. Die praktische Spracherlernung auf Grund der
Psychologie und der Physiologie der Sprache. 3rd ed.

Fries, Charles C. 1945. The teaching and learning of English as a
foreign language. Ann Arbor, University of Michigan.

Gage, N.L. 1964. Handbook of research on teaching. Chicago,
McNally.

Ganss, George, S.J. 1956. Saint Ignatius' idea of a Jesuit university.
Milwaukee, Marquette University Press.

Gauntlett, J.O. 1957. Teaching English as a foreign language. London,
Macmillan.

Geddes, J. 1933. The old and the new. French Review VII, 1.

Geerts, V.M. and L. Missinne. 1964. La méthode Jacotot pour
l'apprentissage de la lecture et des langues étrangeres était-elle
originale? La nouvelle revue pédagogique XIX, 9.

Gouin, Francois. 1880. L'art d'enseigner et d'étudier les langues.
Paris.

———. 1892. The art of teaching and studying languages. Translated
by Howard Swan and Victor Betis. London, G. Phillip.

———. n.d. Erstes Übungsbuch für das Deutsche.

Gratten, J.H.G. and P. Gurrey. 1929. Our living language. London,
Nelson.

Hamilton, James. 1816. Essay on the usual mode of teaching language.
New York.

———. 1829. The history, principles, practice and results of the
Hamilton System for the last twelve years. Manchester.

Heness, Gottlieb. 1867. Der Leitfaden für den Unterricht in der
deutschen Sprache. New York, H. Holt & Company. Boston,
C. Schönhof. [1884?]

Hermann, Alfred. 1956. Dolmetschen im Altertum. University of
Mainz.

Jacotot, Joseph. 1823. Enseignement universel, langue maternelle. Dijon.

——. 1824. Enseignement universel, musique, dessein et peinture. Paris.

——. 1830. Enseignement universel, langue étrangere. Paris.

——. 1841. Enseignement universel, mathémathiques. Paris.

——. ? Enseignement universel, droit et philosophie panécastique. Paris.

——. 1841. Enseignement universel, mélanges posthumes. Paris.

Jeanes, R. W. 1964. Recent advances in modern language teaching in Canada. Advances in the teaching of modern languages, ed. by R. Libbish. Oxford, Pergamon.

Jespersen, Otto. 1894. Progress in language.

——. 1897-99. Fonetik. Copenhagen.

——. 1901. Fransk Begynderbog. 3rd ed. Copenhagen.

——. 1903a. Kortfattet engelsk grammatik for tale-og skriftsproget. 4th ed. Copenhagen.

——. 1903b. The England and America reader. Copenhagen.

——. 1904. Lehrbuch der Phonetik. Leipzig.

——. 1904-1947 ff. Modern English grammar. 7 vols. London, Allen & Unwin. 1954.

——. 1905. Growth and structure of the English language. London, Blackwell.

——. 1922. Language, its nature, development, and origin. New York, Macmillan. 1949.

——. 1924. Philosophy of grammar. New York, H. Holt & Co.

——. 1925. Mankind, nation and individual from a linguistic point of view. Cambridge, Harvard University Press. (University of Indiana Press, 1965).

——. 1930. Novial lexike. London, G. Allen & Unwin.

——. 1933a. Essentials of English grammar. New York, H. Holt & Co.

——. 1933b. A system of grammar. London, G. Allen & Unwin.

——. 1933c. Linguistica: selected papers in English, French and German. London, G. Allen & Unwin.

——. 1938. En sprogmands leoned. Copenhagen.

——. 1947. How to teach a foreign language. London, G. Allen & Unwin.

——. 1960. Selected writings. London, G. Allen & Unwin.

Jespersen, Otto, with Chr. Sarauw. 1902-3. Engelsk Begynderbog, I-II. 3rd ed. Copenhagen.

Jones, Daniel, 1909. Pronunciation of English. Cambridge, Cambridge University Press.

——. 1922. An outline of English phonetics. Leipzig, Teubner.

Jones, Daniel. 1937. An English pronouncing dictionary. New York, Dutton.

———. 1950a. The phoneme, its nature and use. Cambridge, Heffer.

———. 1950b. Harold E. Palmer (1877-1949). Le maitre phonétique 93.

Kahl, P. Wilhelm. 1962. Muttersprache und Fremdsprache im Englischunterricht der Volks- und Mittelschulen. Part A (historische Entfaltung des Problems). Weinheim, Beltz.

Klinghardt, H. 1888. Ein Jahr Erfahrungen mit der neuen Methode. Marburg.

———. 1892. Drei weitere Jahre Erfahrungen. Marburg.

Kramer, S.N. 1956. From the tablets of Sumer. Indian Hills, Colorado, The Falcon's Wing Press.

———. 1963. The Sumerians: their history, culture, and character. Chicago, The University Press.

Kron, R. 1895 (2nd ed. 1900). Die methode Gouin oder das Serien-system in theorie und praxis. Marburg.

Lado, Robert. 1964. Language teaching: a scientific approach. New York, McGraw-Hill.

Lado, Robert and J. Ornstein. 1967. Research in foreign language teaching methodology. International review of applied linguistics 5:11-26.

Landré, Louis. 1965. François Closset (1900-1964). Les langues modernes 59.

Lehmann, Alwin. 1904. Der neusprachliche Unterrricht im 17. und 18. Jahrhundert, insbesondere seine Methode im Lichte der Reform der Neuzeit. Jahresbericht der Annenschule zu Dresden-Altstadt. Dresden.

Leif, J. and G. Rustin. 1953. Pédagogie génerale par l'étude des doctrines pédagogiques. Paris.

Leonard and Cox. 1925. General language.

Leroy, A. 1863. Étude historique et critique sur l'enseignement élémentaire de la grammaire latine. Revue de l'instruction pub-lique en Belgique. Bruxelles.

Libbish, B. ed. 1964. Advances in the teaching of modern languages. New York, Macmillan.

Lindquist, Lilly. 1940. General language. MLJ 24:563-7.

Longfellow, Samuel, ed. 1886. Life of Henry Wadsworth Longfellow. 2 vols. Boston.

McClain, William H. 1945. Twenty-fifth anniversary of the Cleveland Plan. French Review 18:197-201.

Mackey, W.F. 1963. Language teaching techniques. Montreal, Longmans.

———. 1965a. Bilingual interference its analysis and measurement. The journal of communication, 15:239-49.

————. 1965b. Method analysis. Monograph series on languages and linguistics 18, ed. by C. K. Kreidler, 149-162. Washington, D. C., Georgetown University Press.

————. 1965c. Language teaching analysis. London, Longmans.

Mallinson, Vernon. 1957. Teaching a modern language. London, Heinemann.

Marcel, Claude. 1853. Language as a means of mental culture and international communication; or the manual of the teacher and learner of languages. 2 vols. London, Chapman and Hall.

————. 1867. The study of languages brought back to its true principles, or the art of thinking in a foreign language. Translated from the French edition. New York, Appleton and Co.

Meidinger, Johann Valentin. 1783. Praktische französische Grammatik, wodurch man diese Sprache auf eine ganz neue und sehr leichte Art in kurzer Zeit gründlich erlernen kann. Metz, Impr. de J. H. Samuel.

Michaud, Joseph François, ed. 1885. Biographie universelle ancienne et moderne... Vol. 11. Paris, Madame C. Desplaces.

Mooijman, J. P., S. J. 1964. Advances in the teaching of a second language in Holland. Advances in the teaching of modern languages, ed. by B. Libbish, 54-65. Oxford, Pergamon.

Morris, I. 1950. The teaching of English as a second language. London, Macmillan.

————. 1951. English by stages. London, Macmillan.

Moulton, William G. 1961. Linguistics and language teaching in the United States (1940-1960). Trends in European and American linguistics 1930-1960, ed. by Mohrmann, Sommerfelt, and Whatmough, 90-109. Utrecht & Antwerp, Spectrum.

National Defense Language Development Program. 1965ff. Completed research studies, and instructional materials. Washington, D. C., U. S. Government Printing Office.

Newmark, Maxim. 1948. Twentieth century modern language teaching. New York, Philosophical Library.

Nilsson, Martin P. 1955. Die hellenistische Schule. Munich, Beck.

Nostrand, H. L. et al. 1965. Research on language teaching: an annotated international bibliography. 2nd rev. ed. Seattle, University of Washington Press.

Ogden, C. K. 1934. The system of Basic English. New York, Harcourt.

————. 1939. Basic step by step. New York, Barnes Noble.

————. 1943. The ABC of Basic English. Rev. ed. New York, Barnes Noble.

Ollendorf, H. S. 1783. Methode, eine Sprache in sechs Monaten lesen, schreiben und sprechen zu lernen. Altenburg, H. A. Pierer.

Palmer, Harold E. 1916. Colloquial English. Cambridge, Eng., W. Heffer & Son.

——. 1917. The scientific study and teaching of languages. Yonkers-on-Hudson, N.Y., World Book Co.

——. 1920. A first course of English phonetics. 2nd ed. Cambridge, Eng., W. Heffer & Son.

——. 1922a. The oral method of teaching languages. 2nd ed. Cambridge, Eng., W. Heffer & Son.

——. 1922b. English intonation with systematic exercises. Cambridge, Eng.

——. 1927. Everyday sentences in spoken English. Cambridge, Eng., W. Heffer & Son.

——. 1931. The principles of romanization with special reference to Japanese. Tokyo, Maruzen.

——. 1934. The principles of English phonetic notation. Tokyo, Institute for research in English teaching.

——. 1938. A grammar of English words. London, Longmans.

——. 1940. The teaching of oral English. London, Longmans.

——. 1948. The five speech-learning habits. Tokyo, Kaitakusha.

——. 1950a. A grammar of spoken English on a strictly phonetic basis. 3rd ed. Cambridge, Eng., W. Heffer & Son.

——. 1950b. A new classification of English tones. 2nd ed. Tokyo, Kaitakusha.

——. 1964. The principles of language-study. London, Oxford University Press.

—— and Dorothee Palmer. 1959. English through actions. London, Longmans.

—— and F.G. Blandford. 1939. Grammar of spoken English on a strictly phonetic basis by Harold E. Palmer, 2nd ed., revised by the author with the assistance of F.G. Blandford.

—— with J. Victor Martin and F.G. Blandford. 1926. A dictionary of English pronunciation with American variants. Cambridge, Eng., W. Heffer & Son.

Passy, P. 1899. La méthode directe dans l'enseignement des langues vivantes. Paris.

Philippine-University of California language program.

Quick, R.H. ed. 1880. Locke on education. London, Cambridge University Press.

——. 1907. Essays on educational reformers. 3rd ed. London.

Renou, L. 1948ff. La grammaire de Pāṇini, traduite du sanskrit avec des commentaires indigènes. Paris.

Report of the committee of twelve of the Modern Language Association of America. 1900. Boston, D.C. Heath & Co.

Richards, I.A. 1943. Basic English and its uses. New York, Norton.

——. 1947. Notes for a discussion of elementary language teaching. Report to UNESCO. Paris.

———. 1952. The new approach to the teaching of language skills as developed by Language Research, Inc. at Harvard University. New York, Seminar Films Inc.

—— and C. M. Gibson. 1943a. Learning the English language. New York, Houghton, Mifflin.

———. 1943b. Words on paper. Cambridge, Mass., Language Research Inc.

———. 1950. A second workbook of English. Cambridge, Mass., Language Research Inc.

———. 1952. English through pictures. New York, Pocket Books, Inc.

Ripman, Walter. 1899. Elements of phonetics. London, Dent & Sons.

—— and Alge. 1898. First French Book. London, Dent & Sons.

Rivers, Wilga M. 1964. The psychologist and the foreign language teacher. Chicago, University of Chicago Press.

Rocklyn, E. H. and W. E. Montague. 1965. A brief review of extreme massing of practice and stress on foreign language acquisition. Human Resources Research Office, Div. No. 7. Alexandria, Va.

Sauveur, L. Causeries avec mes élèves.

———. Petites causeries.

Scherer, G. A. C. and M. Wertheimer. 1964. A psycholinguistic experiment in foreign language teaching. New York, McGraw-Hill.

Sebeok, Thomas A., ed. 1966. Portraits of linguists, 1746-1963. Bloomington, Indiana University Press.

Seidenstücker, Johann Heinrich. 1811. Elementarbuch zur Erlernung der französischen Sprache.

Stack, Edward M. 1964. Advances in language teaching in the United States. Advances in the teaching of modern languages, ed. by R. Libbish, 66-82. London, Pergamon.

Stern, H. H. 1965. Final report on the work of groups and committees. Modern foreign language teaching, ed. by G. Müller, 43-60. Berlin, Cornelsen Verlag.

Strevens, P. 1965. Recent British developments in language teaching. Monograph series on languages and linguistics 18, ed. by C. E. Kreidler, 171-79. Washington, D. C., Georgetown University Press.

Swan, Howard and Victor Betis. 1892. The art of teaching and studying languages, by François Gouin. London, G. Phillip.

Sweet, Henry. 1890. Primer of phonetics. Oxford.

———. 1891. Elementarbuch des gesprochenen Englisch. Oxford.

———. 1893. Anglo-Saxon Primer. Oxford.

———. 1895. Primer of spoken English. Oxford.

———. 1897. First steps in Anglo-Saxon. Oxford.

———. 1900. The history of language. Oxford.

———. 1913. Collected papers of Henry Sweet. Edited by H. C. Wyld.

———. 1964. The practical study of languages. New edition. London, Oxford University Press. (First ed. 1899)

———. 1898. A new English grammar. Oxford. (1958)

Ticknor, George. 1833. Lecture on the best method of teaching the living languages. Boston, Carter, Hendee and Co.
——. 1849. History of Spanish literature. 3 vols. New York, Harper.
Titone, Renzo. 1965. Le lingue estere: metodologia didattica. Rome and Zürich, PAS-Verlag.
Viëtor, Wilhelm. 1884. Elemente der Phonetik des deutschen, englischen und französischen. Leipzig.
——. 1887 and 1893. Phonetische Studien.
——. 1905. Der Sprachunterricht musz umkehren: ein Beitrag zur Überbürdungsfrage. Enlarged and annotated edition. Leipzig.
Villey, Pierre, ed. 1922. Essais de Montaigne. Vol. 1. Paris, Alcan
Walsh, Donald Devenish. 1964. The teaching of modern foreign languages in the United States. Advances in the teaching of modern languages, ed. by R. Libbish, 83-90. Oxford, Pergamon.
Weitenauer, Ignatius. 1762. Hexaglotton sive modus adducendi intra brevissimum tempus linguas: gallicam, italicam, hispanicam, graecam, lusitaneam et syricam. Freiburg (Br.), Wagner.
West, Michael. 1926a. Learning to speak a foreign language.
——. 1926b. Learning to read a foreign language. London, Longmans, Green & Co.
——. 1926c. Bilingualism.
——. 1929. Language in education. London, Longmans.
——. 1935a. Definition vocabulary. Toronto, Dept. of educational resources.
——. 1935b. New method English dictionary. London, Longmans.
——. 1936. Interim report on vocabulary selection. London, King & Son.
——. 1941. Education and psychology.
——. 1951. Improve your English.
——. 1953. General service list of English words. London, Longmans.
—— and Bannerjee. 1936. English words for all occasions. New York, Longmans.
Widgery, W. H. 1888. The teaching of languages in school. London.
Woodward, William Harrison. 1924. Studies in education during the age of the Renaissance, 1400-1600. Cambridge Univ. Press.